Studying God's Word

Studying
God's Word

An introduction to methods of Bible study
Editor: John B. Job
Registrar and Lecturer in Old Testament
at Immanuel College, Ibadan

INTER-VARSITY PRESS

© INTER-VARSITY PRESS, LONDON

Inter-Varsity Fellowship,
39 Bedford Square, London WC1B 3EY

First Edition October 1972

ISBN 0 85110 571 8

Printed in Great Britain by
Hazell, Watson and Viney Ltd,
Aylesbury, Bucks

Contents

In thy commandments I find continuing delight;
  I love them with all my heart.
I will welcome thy commandments,
  and will meditate on thy statutes.

Introduction

Even though this is an age of do-it-yourself (anything from house-building to hair-cutting), it still remains necessary to plead that Christians do Bible study for themselves. The Scriptures certainly provide 'spiritual milk' (1 Pet. 2:2) to build up beginners in the faith, and the young Christian needs help in assimilating the 'milk of the word' in the kind of way that a baby depends on its mother. But when the child comes to tough meat, the days of breast-feeding and spoon-feeding are over. And there is tough meat in the Bible (Heb. 5:12–14), intended for every maturing Christian. It is not there for somebody else to get his teeth into. The command, 'In understanding be men' (1 Cor. 14:20, AV), was addressed not to the theologians of the early church, but to all who would listen.

We need today to recover for the church the kind of passionate involvement in the Bible which has characterized its most effective days. This kind of interest is already apparent within the pages of Scripture itself. Nowhere is it clearer than in Psalm 1, the introduction to the book that served as hymnal both for the church of the Old Testament and for the growing fellowship of the New. There we read that the righteous man is one whose delight is in the law of the Lord. He meditates on it day and night. Elsewhere, Isaiah 31:4, the word for 'meditate' is used of the lion growling over his prey. We should not be surprised therefore to find in another Psalm, 'With open mouth I pant, because I long for thy commandments' and 'I rejoice at thy word like one who finds great spoil' (Ps. 119:131, 162). Indeed anyone ap-

proaching the subject of Bible study could do little better than
read Psalm 119 to discover and be fired by the psalmist's enthu-
siasm for God's Word.

This book is for those who are prepared to see that this kind of
hunger and zest are not, as some would see them, the patho-
logical symptoms of ancient Jewish fanaticism but are the marks
of normal health in the body of Christ. For Jesus Himself shared
this respect and love for the Scriptures, and both before and
after the resurrection He passed on to His disciples that view of
them on which their understanding of Him, and hence their
Christian life and ministry, was founded. We shall see that the
New Testament provides us with ample evidence of this.

The present work originally arose as a response to the need
felt by many who had worked through *Search the Scriptures*[1] for
material to guide them without such a detailed chart in the
exploration of the Bible. Many also who have been accustomed
to using Bible study notes may have a similar urge to supplement
that sort of approach with their own research. Everybody experiences the staleness which comes from settling into the rut of one
particular style of Bible reading. And to some it may come as a
surprise to discover that there are a large number of different
ways of studying Scripture. To adopt a new plan instead of one
that has become too familiar will be refreshing.

We have tried to meet this spectrum of demand, and so not all
chapters will suit all tastes. Temperamentally some readers will
be attracted by an analytical approach (*e.g.* chapters 2, 3, and 5),
and some by a synthetic (*e.g.* 6 and 7) or historical approach
(*e.g.* 4). There are treasures in the Bible which surrender to one
who is prepared to grind small the details of one passage. But
there are too (as Austin Farrer once graphically expressed it)
spiritual sparks which fly when two or more passages of Scripture are, like the proverbial sticks of prehistoric man, rubbed
together.

This is partly why the book has been written as a symposium,
and why the contributors are of various denominations and
trained in various disciplines. The chapters will differ not only
according to their subject-matter, but also in the individual

[1] A. M. Stibbs (ed.), *Search the Scriptures* (Inter-Varsity Press, 1967).

approach of the authors. There will inevitably be differences of
emphasis and shades of interpretation; but the authors are united
in their belief that the Bible is both true and trustworthy, and that
it merits close study. They are also one in emphasizing the
importance of treating biblical revelation as a whole. In a sense
therefore the chapter, *Bible study and unity of the Bible*, could be
seen as the linchpin of the whole book. Individual methods of
Bible study may vary, but attention to the context and the relation
of any particular passage to the whole picture of God's revelation
is crucial.

Each of the first seven chapters deals with one particular
method of Bible study, and includes a worked-out example and
suggestions for further similar studies. Chapters 8 and 9 are
concerned with the *use* of the Bible in approaching specific
problems, both moral and personal. They anwer pressing questions about the relevance of the Bible in everyday living, and try
to show how it can be applied. Clearly they differ in approach
from the more deductive method of the earlier chapters, but
again the interrelation of different methods becomes apparent.
The final chapter is something of an appendix, as it tries to give
some initial answers to a problem all Bible-students must face
the more deeply they study the Bible, the problem of difficult
passages either in terms of morality, history or internal consistency. None of the chapters of course is exhaustive. They attempt
merely to be introductions, from which it is hoped the reader will
continue and find out for himself that God's Word is truth, and
that study of it is an essential part of the training of the complete
man of God (2 Tim. 3:17).

It is no use pretending that Bible study is anything but an
arduous activity. There is a plea in these pages[2] for the learning of
Hebrew; few would regard this as an easy option since it is
obvious that to learn a language requires discipline. But what is
true of learning Hebrew is true to a greater or lesser extent of
any of the techniques suggested here for the deepening of one's
knowledge of the Bible. This can be explained quite simply. To
read a passage in Hebrew is to fix it in one's mind. The sheer
effort of translation makes an indelible imprint on the memory.

[2] See page 58.

The same is true of preaching about a passage. To work out a sermon, if it is properly expository, involves the kind of wrestling with the passage which likewise fixes it in the mind. Mere reading, on the other hand, does not have the same effect. It lacks that marking, learning and inwardly digesting spoken of in Cranmer's prayer. The purpose of Bible study is thus that the message of a particular passage should become part of us. This is our objective in the long run with the Bible as a whole. This aim may be achieved, as we have made clear, in a variety of ways. But it can be achieved only with effort.

On the other hand, it is the note struck by the psalmist that should figure dominantly in any *envoi* for such a book. We can but hope that the same sense of enjoyment as he expresses will be seen to radiate from the contributors. It comes partly from laying bare the riches of the biblical message itself, with all that this offers of hope and encouragement. But it is also the sheer joy of discovery. One thing may be promised with assurance to the person who studies the Bible for himself: he will find out truths about God which nobody has ever told him.

1 Bible Study and the Unity of the Bible

ALEC MOTYER

One book

The words 'Old Testament' are never used by Jesus or His apostles to describe a book. If anyone had gone to Peter at the conclusion of his Pentecost sermon and asked, 'Why do you keep on quoting from the Old Testament?', the response would have been a look of blank incomprehension! Further attempts at clarity would have elicited the reply, 'Oh, I see. You mean the Scriptures.'[1]

Nothing would do more to transform our attitude to the Bible or open up to us more fruitful avenues of reading and study than to forget the false and on the whole unhelpful division into 'Old' and 'New' and to learn from Jesus and the apostles about the one, single book of divine truth graciously given to us. For, without a doubt, this is how the Bible itself would have us think of it. The Lord Jesus is central to the whole, both as its subject matter and also as the divine risen Lord setting the seal of His authority on this book as the sole and essential means of under-

[1] The New Testament describes the Old Testament as 'the law' (*e.g.* Mt. 5:18), a word which, in Hebrew, means 'instruction' rather than 'legislation', and points to the contents of Scripture as the teaching personally imparted by the Lord to His people; sometimes it is called 'the law and the prophets' (*e.g.* Mt. 7:12), or 'Moses and the prophets' (Lk. 24:27), or 'Moses and the prophets and the psalms' (Lk. 24:44) describing the divisions of this revealed material; most frequently the description is 'the scripture' (*e.g.* Jn. 2:22) or 'the scriptures' (*e.g.* Mk. 12:24; 14:49) with the accompanying formula of quotation 'it is written' (*e.g.* Mt. 4:4; Jn. 2:17; 1 Cor. 1:19), indicating the form in which this revealed teaching from God has been preserved for use.

standing Him and His work (Lk. 24:26, 27) and of preaching Him to the world (Lk. 24:44–47). Thus His backward glance authenticates the Old Testament (for, misleading though the term is, convenience dictates that we must continue to use it), and His forward-looking promise (Jn. 14:25, 26) pledges to the apostles a special activity of the Holy Spirit inspiring them in the recollecting of His own teaching, a promise which was fulfilled in the completion and record of the New Testament Scriptures. But the apostles did not consider that they were helping towards the compilation of a 'second' book to add to a 'first', a 'new' to be attached to, even to supersede, an 'old'. Paul bracketed as Scripture the words of Jesus with a quotation from Deuteronomy, thus putting a 'New Testament' passage on the same level as the earlier inspired Word of God (1 Tim. 5:18); likewise he included the teaching which he had deposited with Timothy along with the inherited 'sacred writings' as alike having the divine inspiration which belongs to 'all scripture' (2 Tim. 3:10–17), and Peter can speak of Paul's letters and 'the other scriptures' (2 Pet. 3:15, 16). It is to this totality of Scripture that the promise is attached that it brings the individual to full maturity and is the complete equipment for service (2 Tim. 3:17).

The value of Bible reading

This view of the Bible as a single book has an immediate, practical corollary. In relation to any book which is a true unity the message of the whole emerges as we become more and more acquainted with the contents of each part. This is pre-eminently true of the Bible: not only does one part illuminate another, but the only way to guard ourselves against over-emphasizing one truth or neglecting another is to fit ourselves to be able to see each truth in the context of the whole.

Behind all Bible study in the narrower sense of the term there must be Bible reading in the widest sense of the term: reading which has as its primary, overriding aim the knowledge of the contents of the whole Bible. Does this seem an impossible aim? Is the Bible really too large for us to plan to read it from cover to cover as a regular and repeated exercise? Surely not! One of the most popular bindings of the RSV contains 843 pages in the Old

Testament and 242 pages in New. Reading at the rate of three pages a day will cover the whole Bible in a year.[2] It must be stressed that the object in this scheme of reading is growing familiarity with the contents of the Bible. It is not a hunt for helpful verses (though many will be found), nor does it allow time for the solution of the many problem-passages which will be noted only in passing. Its limited—though magnificent and basic—objective is a gradual and steady raising of the level of Bible knowledge, the essential prerequisite of true study. T. C. Hammond ever gave the same advice to new converts with inimitable vividness: 'Read the Bible in great dollops!' There is no better advice for the Christian who aspires to Bible study.

Taking the long view: project work

Without losing sight of the fact that our reading and re-reading of the Bible aims at increasing mastery of the whole Book, we can in addition harness it to specific study purposes. Our Lord's controversy with the Pharisees over Sabbath-keeping centred on the fact that they based their whole practice on a single item (Ex. 20:10b) in the great richness of the teaching of Scripture about the Lord's day. He was able to point to three relevant Scriptures which they had overlooked (Mt. 12:3, 5, 7). Project work is an attempt to gather the totality of Bible teaching, and here is a truly endless harvest for the student. The best equipment for the task is a smallish loose-leaf notebook. Suppose one were gathering teaching about the Holy Spirit. The first reference to be considered would be Genesis 1:2, the activity of the Spirit of God in creation. The key-word here would be 'creation', and the reference and its teaching would be filed away under the letter 'C'. In the same way each succeeding reference is given to a

[2] Banner of Truth has republished Murray M'Cheyne's scheme for reading the whole Bible once, and the New Testament and Psalms twice, in the course of a single year. The above suggestion of so many pages a day is less sophisticated but much more flexible to individual requirements. No mathematical genius is required to discover how many pages in one's own Bible must be covered to read the Old Testament twice and the New Testament four times in a year—or any other target of reading. Also, within the target adopted, other subdivisions are possible: to include daily some reading from the Gospels, so as to keep the portrait of Jesus ever fresh, is much to be commended.

key-word and filed alphabetically. From time to time the note-book can be reviewed so as to bring the gathering material together under more comprehensive headings. The danger to be avoided is that of being too clever or complicated to start with: much better to let the system grow.[3]

Promise and fulfilment

In one respect the Bible is like a good detective story: clues come first; solutions follow. From the very start the Bible draws the reader on to discover when and how the forecasts it makes will take place. The correspondence of promise and fulfilment belongs to the fabric of Scripture, but this only becomes plain and meaning-ful to the reader who sets out to become aware of the total content of the Bible.

Watch it happening. Abraham is told that his descendants will possess the land (Gn. 15:16–21), and so, indeed, it comes to pass (Jos. 1:1–4). But meantime they have been warned that their tenure was conditional upon obedience and would be forfeited by disobedience (Dt. 28:15ff., 63ff.); this also is fulfilled (2 Ki. 24:1ff.). Yet before the grievous blow of exile falls, a return from exile is promised, and the developing story brings us on to this very point, stressing as it does so the biblical view of history as the successive acts of the God who keeps His word (Ezr. 1:1ff.; cf. Je. 29:10). But there were elements of grandeur about some of the predictions of the return which seemed to be belied by the actual turn of events (e.g. Is. 45:14; cf. Ne. 4:1ff.; etc.). In the complex tapestry of biblical prediction these are not false flashes of brightness; rather we are led to see that there is a Return beyond the return in which all the glory will indeed come to pass. In the teeth of the disappointment, Haggai reaffirms the golden promises (2:3–9), casting their fulfilment yet further forward. In this way they are transformed, by association with the person and work of Jesus, into the vision of the gathering of a world-wide church (Eph. 2:11–22; 1 Pet. 2:4–10) and finally the

---

[3] A loose-leaf page, 7 in. by 4½ in., is easy to come by and a very good size for this kind of note-taking. It is large enough for the longer note and small enough to be devoted to a single comment without waste. For topics which lend themselves to this kind of study see chapter 6, *Theme Study.*

assembling of the redeemed in heaven (Rev. 7:9) among which, answering Haggai's vision, the nations shall walk and to which the kings of the earth shall bring their glory (Rev. 21:24).

One who reads through the Bible looking for promises and their fulfilment will gather a rich harvest. Central to this theme are the chapters of Isaiah, 40–48, which insist that the distinctive mark of the God of the Bible is that He speaks and brings to pass, He promises and fulfils. This is one of the Bible's own 'proofs of the existence of God'.

Word study

A growing awareness of the unity of the Bible promotes confidence in the belief that it will use its distinctive terminology in a consistent and illuminating fashion. Procedurally, the method here is the same as in the case of project work except that one can cut a very long corner by using a concordance.[4] This is not only a fascinating form of Bible study in its own right, but is an essential method for arriving at a truly biblical definition of the meaning of key words and ideas.

Five aspects of relationship

The distinction between Old and New Testaments is so rooted in our minds that it is easiest at this point to say that there are (at least) five aspects of the relationship between the Testaments. Nevertheless there is no harm in reminding ourselves that we should rather speak of the five ways in which the unity of the Bible unfolds itself. The five are as follows: *confirmation, i.e.* the unfolding of truth in the Bible, and especially the normative words and deeds of Jesus, confirm earlier lines of revelation; *finalization, i.e.* where the earlier revelation has embedded the truth in provisional forms, guarded it by temporary safeguards, or couched it in contemporary but ultimately inadequate thought-forms, it is then stated in its final form; *dependence, i.e.* the final statement of a truth assumes all that has gone before and cannot be understood without reference to the earlier words or events; *reaffirmation, i.e.* some items in the Old Testament seem at first

4 See Chapter 5, *Word study*, particularly p. 59 and footnote.

sight to be out of step with the character of Jesus and the revelation vouchsafed in Him, yet the New Testament does not reject but reaffirms them; *completion, i.e.* the Bible expresses a progressive revelation, an accumulating body of truth in which the New Testament rounds out the Old.

1. Confirmation

In offering now a brief treatment of each of these five in turn, it is quite helpful to start our consideration of confirmation by thinking of the Bible as the book which 'provides anwers at the back': the exactness of our understanding of the Old Testament is revealed when we find our conclusions confirmed by positive New Testament statements. Suppose we ask, for example, how we are to understand those Old Testament references which appear to forecast the coming of a *divine* Messiah? This seems to be the implication of the titles, 'Immanuel' (Is. 7:14), 'the Lord our righteousness' (Je. 23:6) and 'the arm of the Lord' (Is. 53:1); the Messiah seems clearly to be called 'God' in Psalm 45:6 and 'Lord' in Malachi 3:1. Yet can we believe that Old Testament believers really expected an incarnation? Certainly, if they did, such expectation had been lost among the Jews of the time of Jesus! But Jesus Himself confirms this line of interpretation (by His question in Lk. 20:44), and in so doing stands inside the uniform New Testament position on the point.

EXAMPLES FOR STUDY
The following line of references may suggest avenues of study on this question: Psalm 2:7 (*cf.* Acts 13:33; 1:4; Heb. 1:5; 5:5); Isaiah 4:2 (not the same word for 'branch' as in Je. 23:5, *cf.* Je. 33:15; Zc. 3:8; 6:12, but the same idea to point to divine 'ancestry'); Isaiah 7:14; 9:6, 7 (where human and divine are combined, *cf.* Mt. 1:18ff.; Lk. 1:35; Jn. 1:14; 6:41–51; 8:53–59; 10:30–36; Gal. 4:4–7); Psalms 45:6, RSV mg.; 110:1; Malachi 3:1 (*cf.* Jn. 20:28; Rom. 9:5, RSV mg.; Tit. 2:13; Heb. 1:1–3).

Another line of enquiry into the way in which the Bible at length confirms its interpretation of itself concerns the significance of 'blood' in sacrifice. The interpretation which affords a coherent account of the evidence is that which sees the blood as proof of a life terminated by death, and, more specifically, a substitutionary death. This is exemplified in Exodus 12:13; Leviticus 17:11; Isaiah 53:4, 5, 11, 12; Mark 10:45; John 10:14, 15; Romans 3:23–25; Galatians 3:13; 1 Timothy 2:5, 6; Hebrews 9:11–22; 10:1–14; 1 Peter 1:18, 19.

2. Finalization

The Old Testament sounds rather strange in our ears when it prohibits wearing 'a mingled stuff, wool and linen together' (Dt. 22:11), yet the principle which was there embodied in a form suited to its own time remains in order to be given a final form in the New Testament insistence that the Christian must never treat outward appearance as a matter of indifference or separable from other aspects of personal testimony (1 Cor. 11:4ff.; 1 Pet. 3:3, 4). This comparatively minor matter may serve to illustrate the principle of finalization which marks the Bible.

The principle appears in depth in relation to the central theme of 'law and grace'. On the main issue here the Bible displays an unvaried stance: Mount Sinai was the primary proof that the Lord had been the agent in redeeming His people from Egypt (Ex. 3:12), and consequently the law enunciated from Sinai was not a system of 'works' whereby the unsaved might diligently merit salvation, but was rather given as a pattern of life to those who had already been redeemed by the blood of the lamb (Ex. 6:6, 7; 12:13). The 'balance' of Exodus is exactly matched by the 'balance' of many Pauline epistles: first the display of the fact, richness, wonder and effectiveness of redemption (e.g. Eph. 1–3), and then the outline of the pattern of life God desires in the redeemed (e.g. Eph. 4–6). Yet within this similarity of basic design, a truly radical touch of transformation has descended upon each of the constituent parts, bringing some to a conclusion, relating some to their new context, and reformulating others.

EXAMPLES FOR STUDY

Grace and law

The basic design (above) is that the law provides the pattern for the responsive life of the redeemed. From beginning to end the

Bible bears this out: Genesis 8:18–9:7; Exodus 12:1–20; 13:1–10; 20:1–17; 24:4–8; Leviticus 19; Deuteronomy 4:9–20, 32–40; 6:20–25; 7:6–11; 10:12–11:9; 14:1, 2; 26:1–11; 29:1–13; Joshua 24:1–15; Judges 6:7–10; Psalms 15; 24; 95; 103; 105:26–45; Isaiah 5:1–7; Jeremiah 31:31–34; Ezekiel 20:1–24; 36:22–27; Micah 6:1–8; Matthew 5:1–12; 7:15–27; 21:33–43; Luke 3:7–11; John 15:1–12; Romans 3:19–31; 6:15–23; 7:1–6; 13:8–14; 1 Corinthians 3:10–15; 5:6–8; 2 Corinthians 6:1–7:1; Galatians 5:15–6:10; Ephesians 4:17–32; 5:1–14; Colossians 3:1–17; 1 Thessalonians 4:1–8; Titus 2:11–14; 3:3–8; Hebrews 6:9–12; 10:10–25; James 2:14–26; 1 Peter 1:13–22; 2 Peter 1:1–11; 1 John 1:5–2:6; 3:1–12; *etc.*

Laws brought to a conclusion

One example is the food-laws, which are clearly abrogated in Mark 7:19. What was right and necessary in its own time (Lv. 11, Dt.14:3–21) has no direct application or authority in ours. Yet it was slow to die out (Acts 10:9–16), for which we may be thankful in that it occasioned the sensitive teaching on Christian brotherliness in Romans 14.

A new context

The main element needing re-orientation within the 'law and grace' complex was the mode of individual entrance into the benefits of salvation. Owing to the inevitable repetitiveness of the old sacrifices (Heb. 10:1–4, 11) the individual's response to God's promises of salvation had to be in terms of offering his own sacrifice (Lv. 1–7). The finality of Christ's sacrifice on the cross terminates this sacrificial process and opens up to the individual the avenue of simple responsive faith. Compare the frequent recourse to the provision of the sacrificial system in Psalm 51 (*e.g.* verses 7, 19) with the response indicated in Hebrews 10:10ff. (especially verses 19ff.); Leviticus 5:1–13 with 1 John 1:9–2:2, and Exodus 12: 24–27 with 1 Corinthians 11:23–26.

Further study of the way in which the Bible re-orientates its basic ideas in the light of Jesus Christ can be made in relation to the concepts of kingdom and church. The Old Testament envisages the future of the people of God in its own terms of territorial extension and a perfect priestly organization, while the New Testament teaches us to understand these in terms of missionary expansion and the gathering of a world-wide people under the perfect priesthood of Jesus. Compare Isaiah 9:6, 7; 11:14–16; 45:14–25; Psalm 110; Amos 9:11–15, with John 18:36; Acts 15:14–18; Romans 10:16–20; also Ezekiel 40–48 (especially 43:1–9) with Ephesians 2:11–22, and Exodus 19:4–6 with 1 Peter 2:9, 10.

Reformulated laws

The New Testament never quotes the Fourth Commandment, and this (coupled with, for example, Col. 2:16) suggests the reformulation of the Sabbath idea away from the Pharisaical fixation on the strict terms of Exodus 20:9, 10, but completely within the terms enunciated by Jesus, and well within the principle of the Lord's Day elaborated throughout the Old Testament. See Genesis 2:1ff. (with Ex. 20:11 and Jn. 5:17); Exodus 16:23–30; 31:12–17 (with Ezk. 44:24); Leviticus 23:3 (with 2 Ki. 4:23; Lk. 4:16; Acts 13:14); Deuteronomy 5:12–15 (with Mk. 3:4); Ezekiel 20:12 (with Lk. 4:31; Acts 16:13; 17:2, RSV mg.; 18:4); Isaiah 56:4–8; 58:13, 14; Mark 2:23–3:6 (especially 2:27, 28). *Cf.* Matthew 12:1–6; Romans 14:1–12 (especially verses 5, 6).

3. Dependence

So far we have seen the New Testament confirming lines of Old Testament truth or bringing Old Testament ideas into their final form. But in many instances the New Testament simply assumes the Old Testament position and depends on it to make its own teaching full and clear. A very good example of this is the New Testament's quiet dependence on the doctrine of God the Creator worked out at length in the Old. In the Old Testament, the activity of God the Creator contains four departments: the absolute origin of all things, the maintenance of the created universe, the executive control of the affairs of men and nations, and the guidance of history to its appointed goal in the Messianic kingdom. One of the reasons why the Old Testament is so long and so heavily weighted with history is to give this range of doctrine a chance to display itself and to settle into a pattern. But the New Testament accepts it to the full, in all its parts and in all its implications.

EXAMPLES FOR STUDY

The absolute origin of all in God: Genesis 1:1–2:4; Isaiah 40:12–26; John 1:1–3; Colossians 1:16ff.

The Creator maintains His creation and ordains its history: Isaiah 44:24–28; 54:14–17; John 5:10–18; Hebrews 1:1–3; Acts 4:24–28.

Individual events are ordained by Him: Isaiah 10:5–15; Job 1, 2; Luke 13:1–9; Acts 2:23, 24.

He brings in the appointed Messianic kingdom: Isaiah 4:2–6; Ezekiel 20:1–44; Amos 9:11–15; Mark 13:1–37 (especially verses 32–37); Acts 1:7.

The same topic of dependence may be interestingly studied in the way the New Testament relies on the Old for all the necessary background and foundation for its own sacrificial terminology. In other words, it not only confirms what the Old Testament says about sacrifice and its meaning, but then it assumes all that as true in its own exposition of the death of Christ, using the characteristic ideas of redemption, propitiation (RSV expiation), atonement, reconciliation, forgiveness, *etc.* All these words repay word study.

4. Reaffirmation

The references given immediately above indicating that Old and New Testaments coincide in ascribing direct management of world events to God perfectly illustrate the self-consistency of the Bible. There are at least two main points where the Old Testament could be blandly dismissed as representing something primitive and outmoded, but where, on the contrary, the New Testament sets its seal of approval on the thought-forms involved. It has a true appearance of Christian reasonableness to question if it is possible for us, in the light of Jesus, to accept the Old Testament's testimony to direct, divine acts of executive judgment. Can such an act as the proposed extermination of the Canaanites (*e.g.* Dt. 7:1–3) be in any way associated with 'the God and Father of our Lord Jesus Christ'? Yet, within the Old Testament, this act, dreadful though it is, belongs in the context of Abraham's affirmation that the Judge of all the earth does right (Gn. 18:24) and the Lord's affirmation (prospectively) of the moral rightness and inevitability of His judgment on the peoples of Canaan (Gn. 15:16). The Lord Jesus Himself assumed without question that God continued to exercise the same moral providence over the world in a way that covered both wilful (Lk. 13:1–3) and accidental (verses 4, 5) calamities, clarifying His position by the parable of the fig tree (verses 6–9).

Again, it has the appearance of Christian reasonableness to question if the spirit of the 'imprecatory psalms' (*e.g.* Pss. 109; 137; 139:19–22) is compatible with the spirit of Jesus and should not rather be dismissed as evidencing an 'Old Testament morality' belonging to the past and best forgotten. Yet the New Testament quotes the imprecatory Psalm 69 on five separate occasions, treating it throughout as inspired Scripture, finding in it teaching about Jesus, Judas and those who reject the gospel, and asserting that it expresses what 'the Holy Spirit spoke beforehand by the mouth of David'.[5] Thus the New Testament reaffirms the scriptural reality of a wholly righteous anger.

FURTHER EXAMPLES

On the general question of theodicy, compare Genesis 6:7 with Matthew 24:37–51, where the fact and its meaning are reaffirmed by Jesus, and 2 Peter 3:1–13, where it is integrated into an unchanging picture of divine activity. Compare also 2 Kings 2:23–25[6] with Acts 12:1–24, and Ezekiel 11:1–13 with Acts 5:1–11 – note that in each case the judgment falls on people living in spiritual pretence.

[5] Ps. 69 is quoted by Jesus (Jn. 15:25), the disciples (Jn. 2:17), and Paul (Rom. 15:3) as predicting the experience, activity and character of the Messiah. *Cf.* Acts 1:16–20; Rom. 11:9, 10.

[6] NB 'boys' in verse 23 is used in the Old Testament for people up to the age of forty years, and there is no need to adopt a tendentious and prejudicial translation like 'small boys'. Bethel was the centre of religious apostasy and therefore of opposition to Elisha. Without a doubt, the new prophet was faced with an organized rabble determined to 'see him off'. If forty-two were mauled by the bears, how many got away unscathed? Thank God for the precious truth that God stands by His beleaguered servants!

5. Completion

The words 'progressive revelation' have been clamouring for expression throughout this discussion of the five-fold unity of the Bible. Truth is built upon truth until the completed revelation emerges. In one sense the idea of 'completion' covers all four categories already illustrated; yet it is as well to provide additional examples in which a gradually increasing illumination ends in full noonday.

One such is the question of the nature of life after death. The Old Testament position is to assert the certainty of an after-life for all alike (*e.g.* Gn. 37:35; Ps. 49:7–9; Is. 14:9ff.), to affirm the blessed hope of the people of God (*e.g.* Pss. 16:9, 10; 49:13–15; 73:23, 24), and to view death with fear and alarm and the life to come with darkness and dread, should the person die unfortified by the favour of God (*e.g.* Jb. 17:13–16; Pss. 6:5; 30:9; 88:10–12). It should be noticed that none of these latter verses speak of death in general, but specifically of those who feel themselves to be dying alienated from God's favour.

We have to wait, however, for Jesus and the New Testament to abolish death, and bring life and immortality to light through the gospel (2 Tim. 1:10). But with the revelation of life and light there came (and chiefly on the lips of Jesus) the revelation of darkness and doom. Hell is a distinctively New Testament revelation, part of the completion of truth.

FURTHER EXAMPLES

The New Testament's revelation concerning death and immortality can be followed through further in, *e.g.*, Luke 23:43; John 14:2, 3; 17:24; Acts 7:54–60; 1 Corinthians 15:35ff.; Philippians 1:21–23, *etc.* Concerning judgment and hell, see Matthew 10:28; 18:8; 25:41–46; Romans 2:6–9; 2 Thessalonians 1:8, 9; Revelation 20:11–15, *etc.*

Other topics which may usefully be studied in this context are marriage, divorce, the church, world-wide mission, but above all the deepening revelation of God Himself, noting particularly how the revelation of the divine Name, Yahweh, in its fullness of meaning is linked with the Exodus (Ex. 1–12, especially 3:13–15) and how the greatest emphasis on the Holy Trinity comes in our

Lord's Calvary discourse in John 14–16 (especially 14:16, 26; 15:26; 16:14).

The theme of completion offers endless avenues of fruitful Bible study, but since the same can be said for each of the previous categories the brief illustration already given must be sufficient.

Conclusion

The Christian's aim must always be to become master of biblical knowledge. The five categories outlined above can at first be used as questions, in the manner suggested in Chapter 7, *Root Study*.[7] To work through the examples offered may help to familiarize the reader with this approach. But in the long run everything comes back to one's personal willingness to adopt a 'whole-Bible' reading method (whether the one suggested here, or some other), to be methodical, to keep and systematize notes, but, above all, to toil at the sacred text, a privilege and an endless satisfaction.

[7] See page 81.

2 Analysing a Book

LAURENCE PORTER

The Bible is not an easy book to read, nor indeed should we expect it to be so, since it communicates to us with our limited ability to understand the wisdom of the infinite, omniscient God Himself and His demands upon men. The greatest minds of the ages have devoted themselves to its understanding; after a lifetime of application they still felt themselves as standing merely among the ripples on the shore of a limitless sea. Yet on the other hand the Scriptures are given that all might feed on them, the simplest as well as the scholar and the sage. We may bring to bear upon them all the faculties of intellect and education, whether great or small, that God has blessed us with, or we can read simply to hear the voice of God speaking to our hearts. These two approaches, the ways of study and of devotion, both have their place; they are not alternative but complementary. The more thorough the Bible study, the richer will be the devotional reading that follows.

Why study a book?

In this chapter we are concerned with the former, and with one particular method of study at that. The Bible is not so much a book as a shelf of books coming to us from different periods of history, different conditions of men, varying backgrounds of culture and even of language. These books were gathered together over the years as it was borne in upon men's spirits that they differed from all other human literature in that their *ultimate* author was the Holy Spirit, and that in reading them men encountered the living God. This does not mean that the *immediate* authors, Moses, David, Paul and the rest, were merely passive instruments—they were writers and not typewriters. Inspiration was not mechanical dictation of the kind supposed by many Muslims to have produced Islam's *Koran*. God selected a man and moulded him by appropriate education and searching experience to write what He then put into his heart. The great figure of Moses, who stands behind the *Torah*, the five books of the Law, received his training first in Pharaoh's court and then in the solitude of the edge of the desert. David, the sweet singer of Israel, who in some of his Psalms foreshadows so remarkably the very meditations of the Lord Jesus Himself, learned of the ways of God when he was a fugitive from Saul with a price on his head. Paul, who set forth in his Epistles the new interpretation of the Old Testament scriptures made necessary by their fulfilment in the coming of Christ, was providentially prepared for this mission by long years of training as a Jewish Rabbi, and then the solitude of 'Arabia'. As we read their writings in the Bible we are reading the unmistakable Word of God; yet we cannot but be aware of the personalities of the men God had chosen, trained and equipped. This we shall see much more clearly if we study a whole book as a unit than if we follow a scheme of selected readings, however well chosen.

Further, many of the books have their origin in the context of a particular historical situation. The first part of the prophecy of Isaiah shows how prophet and kings reacted to the imminent peril of Assyrian invasion. Many passages will be misunderstood, or indeed incomprehensible, if wrenched from their context and read in isolation. There are various interpretations of 1 Corinthians 11:1–16; and because our minds are finite and our understandings imperfect, none can claim finality for his own opinion on the matter. But our interpretation will certainly be inadequate unless we have in mind that Paul's primary teaching here was given in reply to the enquiries of a first-century church about its own specific problems. An extreme literalist who taught from this chapter that women must wear *veils* in church would display little understanding of the context! Colossians, again, contains many ideas foreign to our way of thinking; to us it will be in many parts mere rhetoric, especially if we read it in the AV. We shall make heavy weather of understanding what Paul is really getting at unless we know something of the Colossian heresy with which he was dealing. The prologue of the fourth Gospel, even, which can float so comfortably over us at carol services, can be singularly meaningless to us unless we follow its motifs, as John develops them throughout his Gospel, to the great clue to their understanding in 20:31, 'These are written that you may believe ... and that believing you may have life in his name'.

It is clear that for understanding any text of Scripture it must be seen in its context and against the background of the whole document to which it belongs. Accordingly, in his systematic study the Bible student will take as his unit not a reading from a ready-made selection, but a complete document at a time. First, in this way he will become aware of a dimension that selected readings cannot give, namely, perspective. He will be guarded against one of the perils of Bible-reading, lopsidedeness. Most of the heresies that have distressed the church throughout its history have sprung not from the introduction of doctrinal untruth, but from emphasis on one particular biblical doctrine at the expense of others. Further, the whole-book method of study compensates for the selected-passage method which has, in the principle of selection, a human element superimposed upon Scripture.

Definition

There now arises the question of definition: what exactly do we mean by a *single book*? Some literary unities in the Bible extend over more than one of the sixty-six books named on the contents page. Samuel, Kings and Chronicles each form one book in the Hebrew; they were not divided into halves until the Septuagint (Greek version) of the second century BC. The change was dictated by considerations of convenience—the amount of text that could be inscribed on one scroll. In the New Testament the case of Luke and Acts is somewhat similar; the two books tell

one continuous story, though the fact that Acts as well as Luke
has a preface to Theophilus, and that Acts 1:1-12 resumes and
expands some of the material of Luke 24 shows that Acts was a
sequel to a book already written. Thus it is different from cases
mentioned where one book has been dissected by editors.
Where in the New Testament there are pairs of Epistles num-
bered 1 and 2 it is a matter of separate letters written on different
occasions to the same recipients. Sometimes, again, more than
one unit can be discerned in a single book. Without entering on
the thorny question of the authorship of Isaiah, it is quite clear
that in it are two totally distinct collections of Isaiah's prophecies
dealing with different situations separated by nearly two centu-
ries, one over-shadowed by the menace of Assyria, the other
when Assyria has disappeared from the face of history and her
proud successor, Babylon, is on her way out as well.

Aim and methods of analysis

When we have selected the document which is to be the theme of
our study, how are we to set about our task? We can know what
we are looking for only with the help of God's Spirit through
prayer. And there are some further important factors to be borne
in mind.

First, God is the God of history: 'By me kings reign, and
rulers decree what is just' (Pɪ. 8:15). To remember this will
help us greatly in our understanding. It is true that we see God's
hand in creation and in nature, but it is in the providential direction of human affairs that we find the fullest revelation of His
nature and purposes. So we find history and teaching side by side
in the Bible. The Pentateuch recounts the story of the earliest
years of the human race and the biographies of individual leaders
such as Abraham, Joseph and Moses, and includes also the great
corpus of the Mosaic legislation.

The method of presentation of the prophetic books is usually
to report the 'oracles' or sermons of the prophets linked together by explanatory biographical and historical data. We have,
moreover, the historical books to supply the general historical
background to the prophets. To make sure that we understand

the relevance of the one to the other, 'cross-references' are often
supplied in the text (cf. Je. 1:1; 21:1; 24:1; 25:1, etc.). In the
New Testament there is the same combination. In the Gospels,
narrative and teaching are intertwined. The narrative portions in
Acts too not only contain reports of sermons and debates, but
serve as a background for the Epistles.

 In studying one book in its entirety, aided by information
furnished in other parts of the Bible, we both see and hear in its
compass the working of God at one particular point of historical
time. But our interest in history is not merely academic or anti-
quarian; God is an unchanging God and the people we shall meet
in our Bible study we shall find singularly like us, with problems
identical with our own. It is as true today as it was in Jeremiah's
day that 'the heart is deceitful above all things, and desperately
corrupt' (Je. 17:9); and the vivid pictures of the eighth century
in Amos and of the bustling world of the Roman empire in Acts
will make our study of the Bible living and contemporary.

Other books of the Bible are devoted to the straightforward
exposition of doctrine. The Epistles of Paul spring immediately
to mind and the other New Testament letters, especially perhaps
Hebrews. In the Old Testament we might think of Proverbs and
Job, though it is interesting to observe that Job, full of teaching
and doctrinal disputation as it is, has this didactic material set
within the life-situation of one man. In some ways straightforward doctrinal material presents fewer difficulties. We may
not find abstract reasoning too easy to follow, but at least we are
not up against any problem concerning the form of literature.
With close application and concentration we shall get nearer to
understanding what the book is seeking to communicate to
us.

A third type is the literature of worship, of which the outstanding example is naturally the book of Psalms. But beside the
Psalms there are many other parts of the Bible where eternal
truths about God are expressed in poetic form. Such are the song
of Miriam and Moses in Exodus 15:1–21, the laments of David
over Saul and Jonathan (2 Sa. 1:19–27) and Absalom (18:33),
the Christological hymn of Philippians 2:5–11, the great
choruses of Revelation, and whole chapters of the prophets.

a. Type of literature

It is important in the interpretation of Scripture to pay attention to the *genre* or type of literature concerned. When reading the poetic portions, the *form* in which things are said is of great importance. Hebrew poetry had no rhyme like ours, but it has a characteristic called *parallelism*, various patterns of repetition of words and ideas, which has the great advantage of not disappearing in translation as rhyme does. Sometimes, recognition that a particular passage is poetry rather than prose will greatly help in understanding it.

Genesis 1 produces interesting results when so examined; the RSV divides its account of creation (verses 2–31) into six paragraphs corresponding with the six days which share a remarkable similarity of pattern. Each contains the same frame-work of phrases: 1 'And God said, "Let . . ."'; 2 'And it was so' (except days 5 and 6); 3 'And God saw that it was good' (except days 1 and 2); 4 'And there was evening and there was morning, a first (second, third, *etc.*) day'. This symmetry, especially when we notice the correspondence between day 1 and day 4, day 2 and day 5, day 3 and day 6, seems to imply that here we are dealing with a hymn of creation rather than a scientific treatise, though we shall not forget that the language of religion is not necessarily less truthful than that of the science text-book. We must know what we are looking for! In discussing one chapter of Genesis we are not deserting our theme of the study of a whole book: Genesis contains many different *genres*.

b. Structure

A second rule of study is that we must understand the *structure* of the book with which we are concerned. F. E. Marsh said the 'structure indicates that which is constructed, as a building, a machine, a bridge; hence, the relative parts which go to make up the whole'. If a future archaeologist came upon the remains of one of these he could learn much. The materials of which it was made, the over-all plan on which it was constructed, its component parts and the manner in which they were assembled, would answer his questions as to what it was all for. The various books of the Bible are equally inter-locking parts of God's self-revelation, but they are constructed in widely differing ways, and a study of these structures will give the careful student valuable clues as to what he must look for.

Sometimes this will present little difficulty; in Hebrews, for example, the writer is careful to make clear the progression of his argument. Sometimes the repetition of a verbal formula at significant points furnishes a helpful clue to the structure. The oracles of the second part of Isaiah (chapters 40–66), for instance, fall naturally into three fairly equal groups of nine chapters each. The dividing verses between the sections (48:22; 57:21) each tell us that God says 'There is no peace for the wicked'. Again, the ministry of Jesus recorded in Matthew's Gospel is set out in five 'books', each ending with the formula, 'When Jesus had finished these sayings (parables)' (Mt. 7:28; 11:1; 13:53; 19:1; 26:1). Elsewhere a particular word or phrase runs through a book, binding it together. In Philippians 'mind', 'joy', and above all 'Christ' are such words, and the study of these words will help us to get the book into focus. An analysis of the letter based on what Paul says about Christ has been suggested:

Chapter 1—Christ our Life (1:21)

Chapter 2—Christ our Example (2:5)

Chapter 3—Christ our Ambition (3:8–9)

Chapter 4—Christ our Satisfaction (4:19).

It is important that we should learn to make our own analyses. This will not usually come easily at first, but some help can be found in books like commentaries and Bible handbooks.[1] Here two points need to be remembered.

First, a ready-made summary is useful as a guide and an aid, but it is no real substitute for the result of our own hard work and understanding. The analysis we make of a Gospel, Epistle or Old Testament book will not reach the same theoretical standard of excellence as that supplied by a dedicated and experienced professional Bible scholar, but for our purpose no summary can be of such value as one worked out by our own study of the text, whatever aids we may have used.

[1] *e.g.* D. Guthrie, J. A. Motyer, *The New Bible Commentary Revised* (Inter-Varsity Press, 1970); R. K. Harrison, *Introduction to the Old Testament* (Tyndale Press, 1970); D. Guthrie, *New Testament Introduction* (Tyndale Press, 1970).

Secondly, in our studies we should not despise the help proffered by writers who are not of our own outlook. Men of all denominations and schools of thought have devoted their lives to the study of the Word of God and have placed the rich harvest of their studies at our disposal. We may disagree with them on important matters, but this should not prevent us from learning from their insights and interpretations.

An example: Mark

It remains only to indicate how these various suggestions might help in the study of an actual text; let us take Mark, the shortest of the Gospels.

First, as to the historical background we have mentioned. The commentaries will point us to other scriptures which show that the author was at the heart of things before the crucifixion, that he later worked with both Paul and Peter, becoming an especially close associate of the latter. His account is clearly based on reliable eye-witness testimony. Chapter 13 gives the impression that the Temple was still standing when Mark wrote; if this is so he was probably nearer to the events than were the other Evangelists.

As to the structure of the Gospel, it was once regarded as an artless stringing together of incidents; later it came to be realized that there was more to it. The Clarendon Bible (1929) says: *'Until Jerusalem is reached,* the gospel is only a series of anecdotes' (*Mark,* p. 35). Now, however, Mark is seen as a carefully composed manual for preachers. As we read (and we should always begin the study of a fresh book by reading it through several times over without any commentary) we shall see several themes. First the very frequent use (over forty times) of a word variously rendered 'immediately', 'forthwith', 'straightway', suggesting the *immediate obedience* of the Servant to His orders. Then there is the idea of *authority*—Jesus acting with authority, and the Jewish leaders challenging His authority both in the earlier and in the final chapters. His authority to call, equip and commission His apostles. We shall note also, on an average more than once per
(*continued on page* 34)

The Gospel of Mark

PROLOGUE 1:1-15

Introduction (1)
Baptism (2-11)
Temptation (12-13)
Beginnings (14-15)

THE SERVANT WHO SERVES 1:16-8:26

1. The Servant appears
Five claims to authority
1:16-45
Authority concerning:
a. discipleship (16-20)
b. teaching (21-22)
c. evil spirits (23-28)
d. sickness (29-34)
e. leprosy (40-45)

The source of His authority
(35-39)

2. The Jews react
Five conflict stories
2:1-3:5
Conflict over:
a. forgiveness (1-12)
b. social convention (13-17)
c. fasting (18-22)
d. the Sabbath day (23-28)
e. the Law (3:1-5)

3. Results of opposition
3:6-5:43
Jesus acts to safeguard
the future of His mision
through:
a. open-air preaching (6-12)
b. disciples' call (13-21)
c. new relationships (22-35)
d. teaching by parables
(4:1-34)
e. search for privacy
(4:35-5:43)

4. Training the disciples
6:1-8:26
Jesus
a. send them out to preach
(1-13)
b. hears of the forerunner's
death (14-31)
c. spreads the Messianic
banquet (32-56)
d. recapitulates (7:1-8:21)
e. heals the blind (22-26)

PETER'S CONFESSION 8:27–30

Having led His disciples to see that He *is* the Messiah, Jesus now teaches them *what kind* of Messiah He is—one who suffers.

THE SERVANT WHO SUFFERS 8:31–15:41

1. The doctrine of the cross
8:31–10:52
a. First prediction of His passion (31–38)
b. Transfiguration (9:1–13)
c. The impotent disciples (14–29)
d. Second prediction of His passion (30–50)
e. Divorce, pride and riches (10:1–31)
f. Third prediction (32–45)
g. Bartimaeus healed (46–52)

2. The crisis of the ministry
11:1–13:37
a. The presentation of Zion's King, *cf.* Zc. 9:9 (1–11)
b. Domination of the Temple (12–26)
c. Attempts to undermine His authority (27–33)
d. Parable of the vineyard (12:1–12)
e. More attempts (13–44)
f. The kingdom of God and the Son of Man (13:1–37)

3. The final hours
14:1–15:47
a. Passover and Last Supper (1–31)
b. Gethsemane (32–52)
c. Jewish trial and denial (53–72)
d. Roman trial (15:1–13)
e. Golgotha (14–41)
f. Entombment (42–47)

EPILOGUE 16:1–20

The empty tomb (1–8)
The risen Lord (9–18)
Ascension and heavenly session (19–20)

chapter, the word *King* or *kingdom*. The majestic figure of the King moves steadily through the first half to the great climax of Peter's recognition of His Messiahship in 8:29.

But He then immediately tells His disciples that He must suffer and even die (8:31). Over the second half looms the shadow of the cross, first our Lord's predictions in sayings (8:31; 9:31; 10:32–34, 45, *etc.*) and parables (*e.g.* 12:1–12), and also in the increasing hostility and machinations of His foes. So we can see a regular pattern in the narrative, summarized in Jesus' own saying: 'The Son of man also came not to be served but to serve, and to give his life as a ransom for many' (10:45). There is the Gospel's theme: the Servant who serves (up to 8:29), the Servant who suffers (8:30 to the end). There also is the answer to Mark's unspoken question, 'Why should One so good and so compassionate be crucified?' It was 'as a ransom for many'.

A detailed analysis of Mark (see pages 32 and 33) may make this clearer. But enough may have been said to indicate the possibilities of spiritual benefit and real enjoyment opened up by the diligent study of one single book of the Bible.

3 Analysing a Passage
JEAN RUTHERFORD

'Love the Lord with all your mind'—part of the supreme summary of the Law, with which Jesus once answered a lawyer's test question (Lk. 10:25ff.). It is our minds, as well as spirit and will, which are needed in analysis of any Biblical passage. Lack of spiritual life leads to dry academic discussion; lack of mental discipline and hard thinking leads to 'beautiful thoughts' floating in a void and to an unbalanced view of God's truth; lack of will makes the whole operation sterile, since the object of Bible study is to help us to discern God's will and His purpose for us, and then to obey Him. Bearing in mind, then, the absolute necessity for the help of the Spirit in all our study and in our practical living out of what we learn, this section is limited to a discussion of the tools to help us understand a given passage.

First assessment

The first essential is to read the passage through slowly and carefully in its entirety several times, before beginning to look at details. It may be helpful heie, if access to various translations is possible, to read the passage in several versions to ensure a good grasp of the main theme. Once this has been done one can then begin a detailed examination of the text.

Pencil and paper certainly help to give form to thought, so the next stage is to work through the passage making notes as one goes. Reviewing these notes afterwards, one can begin to assess

otal picture and the development, or the faceted illustration,
theme. Ultimately the reader may be able to build up his own
of mini-commentaries.

It is essential to clarify the type of passage before proceeding
to detailed study. There is an obvious difference in approach for
poetry and prose, history and argument. Particularly when
handling a poetic passage one needs to beware of too pedes-
trian an approach. The literal meaning may often be nonsense.
Take such a passage as Psalm 60:7f. This does not mean that the
Jews pictured God as washing His hands in Moab. The imagery
is a vivid way of illustrating God's victory and sovereignty.

Detailed study

a. Main theme
Once one has established whether one is dealing with a factual
narrative, a doctrinal exposition, or a poetic account of inward
experience, one can begin to work out the contents of the passage
and the lessons which it teaches, and to ask oneself what would
make a good single sentence to sum up the passage.

b. Principal divisions
English versions of the Bible mark paragraphs. But why are the
paragraph divisions where they are? Sir Ernest Gowers in *Plain
Words* says, 'The paragraph is essentially a unit of thought.'
Paragraph analysis is therefore a search for the key ideas in a
passage. But then, of course, it is possible to subdivide further
on the same principle, to find paragraphs within paragraphs. This
is a fruitful technique to apply particularly to the kind of close
reasoning found in Paul's letters.

c. Links
The links between paragraphs are of vital importance. Too often
Scripture is regarded as a ragbag of individual texts rather than
material which is close-knit, with definite growth and development of ideas from one passage to the next, or from one book to
the next. Scripture is a growing tree rather than a mosaic of unconnected elements.

d. Illustrations

Vivid imagery is one way of focusing the attention on difficult abstract ideas. Our Lord in His parables uses imagery, often very homely imagery, to convey most profound spiritual truths. In some cases the Bible contains its own interpretation. Where this is not the case, care must be taken to understand imagery according to principles which Scripture lays down or illustrates.

e. Repetition

Parallelism, presenting the same idea in two or three different ways, is a fundamental technique of Hebrew poetry and it occurs continually in the Psalms (*e.g.* 59:1). Repetition may be used simply for emphasis, as in our Lord's use of 'Truly, truly, I say to you', or to drive a point home. As any good teacher knows, repetition is necessary as an aid to understanding. For instance, the feeding of the five thousand is in all four Gospels, bringing this important event again and again to our attention. It looks back to the feeding of the Israelites in the wilderness with manna; it looks forward to the Messianic banquet at the end of time, and it speaks of Christ's feeding of us now. So rich an event would obviously be central in the Evangelists' thinking.

f. Key words

Here it would be helpful to refer to the chapter on word study, where there is a full treatment of this important subject.[1]

g. Characters

Somebody is named in the passage we are considering. What else is there about the person in the Bible? Perhaps the point of a passage is made by a contrast between the characters depicted. Obvious examples would be the Pharisee and the tax-collector in Jesus' parable, or the two thieves in Luke's account of the crucifixion. But is there a more subtle contrast to be discerned?

h. Questions

Often the crucial question suggested by a passage will be the main theme. But in any case, it is a good idea to note not only the

[1] See pages 54ff.

questions on which the passage touches, but also the questions which the passage raises in one's mind as one reads it. Are there answers to any of these questions in the passage? It is helpful to contrast such answers with those commonly given in the world around us.

i. Cross-references

For a full treatment of possibilities under this heading, see the chapters on the unity of the Bible and root study.[2]

j. Literary features

Particularly in the poetry, but also in such artistic prose as the story of Joseph, aspects of the meaning of a passage are conveyed not only by what is said but also by how it is said. We need therefore to be on the look-out for unusual word-order or rhythm, and to note the figures of speech and imagery used.

Once this detailed work is completed and a good grasp of the content and aim of a passage has been obtained, one can begin to look at it both in its immediate context, of the particular chapter or book, and then in the wider context of the whole revelation of God in Scripture. It is very necessary to do this further work, so that one does not lose the balance of the whole of Scripture. Much of the New Testament, for example, is written assuming the acceptance of Old Testament teaching. Equally the Old Testament is fulfilled and enriched by the New Testament's definitive revelation in Jesus Christ.

The following sections show the method suggested above applied to three very different types of passage.

Passages for analysis

1. Psalm 73[3]

A. MAIN THEME
The prosperity of the wicked

[2] See pages 11ff. and 74ff.
[3] This study is based on the text of the Jerusalem Bible.

B. DIVISIONS

1. Affirmation about God (1): God is good, the rewarder of the pure.

2. The problem created for the psalmist (2, 3). If v. 1 is true, why do the wicked prosper?

3. The career of the wicked (4–9).

4. Attitude of Israel, God's people (10–12): distorted picture of God, because they look at man.

5. Attitude of psalmist (13–16): puzzled but persevering.

6. The end of the wicked (17–22) as God sees them.

7. The end of the righteous (23–26) as God sees them.

8. Conclusion (27, 28)—personal committal to God, and public witness.

C. LINKS

1. Stark contrast between affirmation about God in 1 and how the psalmist feels in 2, 3.

2. Contrast marked by repetition in 4, 5, 'for them'; by 'after all, why should I?' (13) and 'whereas' (28).

3. 'Instead' (16) marks progress of thought and effort.

4. 'Until' (17) marks break-through and understanding.

5. 'Until, when' (19, 20) are temporal conjunctions indicating ultimate end of wicked.

6. 'Even so' (23): in spite of the psalmist's stupidity he remained in God's presence and God's mercy upheld him.

7. 'Now' (24): present and continuing attitude of trust.

8. 'So then' (27) summarizes whole of preceding argument. In contrast with the passage in Mark 8 (see below) there are many link words which show how carefully the psalmist has thought out his problem and the solution, beginning, continuing and ending in God.

Note too that together with the careful reasoning there is also confident trust and spontaneous warmth of affection from 25 to the end.

D. ILLUSTRATIONS

Verses 6, 7: vivid picture language.

20: simile—note forceful image of 'phantoms', *i.e.* not men.

26: metaphor of rock—contrast with 'slippery slope' of 18.

E. REPETITIONS

Many examples; as we have seen, parallelism is a basic principle
of Hebrew poetry (11, 12). Piled up questions catch the tone of
speech exactly. Note the order, rhythm and balance in building
up to the terrifying climax in 17–20, where the fate of the wicked
is described.

> 'Until the day *I pierced the mystery*'
> '*And saw the end* in store for them:'
> 'they are on *a slippery slope*, you put them there,'
> 'you urge them on *to ruin*,'
> 'Until suddenly *they fall*,'
> 'done for, *terrified to death*.'
> 'When you wake up, Lord, *you shrug them off*'
> 'like the *phantoms* of a morning *dream*.'

The cumulative effect is quite shattering, deftly conveying the
tremendous impact of understanding on the psalmist: 'I pierced
the mystery'.

F. AND G. KEY WORDS (AND CHARACTERS)

Good and wicked: examine their lives, the general opinion the
world has of them, and their end, seen in the light of God's
assessment of them.

H. QUESTIONS

The problem of the wicked who get off apparently scot-free and
prosper and of the innocent who suffer. The answer is seen in
seeing God and in the ultimate end of man.

I. CROSS-REFERENCES

Compare the book of Job, and Psalm 49.

J. LITERARY FEATURES

Through the order of the poem and its emotional force (because
it is very personal in tone), we share the psalmist's agony of mind
and triumphant joy of his 'piercing of the mystery'. The effect
through the poetic form is much more immediate and has greater
impact than cold reasoned argument, for this is a theme on
which people feel strongly.

2. Mark 8[4]

A. MAIN THEME
Sight and blindness

B. DIVISIONS
1. Feeding of the four thousand (1–10)
2. The Pharisees (11–13)
3. The disciples (14–21)
4. The blind man (22–26)
5. Peter's affirmation (27–33)
6. Jesus, and His relationship with disciples and people (34–38)

C. LINKS
1. Then (11)
2. Now (14)
3. Then (34)
   With Mark's usual breathless haste the links are few!

D. ILLUSTRATIONS
1. Leaven (15)
2. Bread (17)
3. The cross (34)

E. REPETITION
1. Action (19, 20)
2. Words (17–21)
3. Questions (27–29, 36–37)

F. CHARACTERS
1. The Pharisees
2. The disciples
3. The blind man
4. Peter

G. KEY WORDS
The words listed above under D. are all suitable candidates for
word study.

---

[4] This study is based on the text of the NEB.

S.G.W–3.

H. QUESTIONS

The important questions raised by the passage are, 'What does blindness signify for the writer at this point? What is the significance of the blind man's partial recovery?' Notice how the narrative of the healing of the blind man focuses and clarifies the preceding and following passages. This shows the importance of studying in context and not in isolation.

Now one can return to the main theme and show how the whole chapter is a commentary on sight and blindness in relation to Jesus. Those with physical sight saw least spiritually; the physically blind man discerned the power of Jesus most clearly. Peter recognized the person of Jesus, but then slipped back and refused to give his obedience to an aspect of God's will which did not suit him. The true vision of Jesus results in a life of obedience which follows Him in the path of self-denial. Further study—Jesus versus the Pharisees in the Gospels. See the chapters which deal with this subject in John Stott's *Christ the Controversialist*.[5]

3. Ephesians 2[6]

A. MAIN THEME
God's salvation

B. DIVISIONS
(The first section is dealt with in detail)

1. *The great transition* (1–5)

When one examines these verses closely, the first thing to emerge is that three parties are spoken of: 'You', 'We' and 'God'. Ask then what is said about each of the three, and note each point on a separate line. The following pattern then presents itself:

i. Time was when *you*	(a) were dead (1)
	(b) followed . . .(2)
	(c) obeyed . . . (2)
ii. *We too*	(a) lived . . . (3)
	(b) obeyed . . . (3)
	(c) lay under . . . (3)

[5] J. R. W. Stott, *Christ the Controversialist* (Tyndale Press, 1970).
[6] This study is based on the NEB text.

iii. But *God*   (a) rich in mercy (4)

                         (b) for the great love he bore us (4)

                         (c) brought us to life (5)

This scaffolding can then be used to support further detailed analysis. In seeking this sort of basic pattern, look first for the conjunctions which are signposts to the structure, and group verbs according to their subjects. Find phrases which are contrasted, or parallel, or in series, whether grammatically or according to the sense, and write them one underneath the other. Have the broad divisions marked out in the left hand margin, and then fill in the details from left to right (as above) to clarify the structural pattern.

2. *God's role* (6–10)

3. *Unity of Jew and Gentile* (11–18)
   i) Disunity (11, 12)
   ii) Reconciliation (13–18)

4. *Growing together* (19–22)

C. LINKS

1. 'But God' (4) marks the contrast between past and present.
2. 'For' (8) explains how the reason for the transition lies in God's action, not ours.
3. '... then' (11) sums up the whole of the previous section.
4. 'But now' (13) marks a contrast parallel to that in verse 4.
5. 'for' (14)
6. 'so' (17)
7. 'For' (18): again the reason lies in God's act.
8. 'Thus' (19)

   Note the complexity of the sentence structure, and the use of both contrast and repetition.

D. ILLUSTRATIONS

1. Death (spiritual) (1)
2. Life (5)
3. Covenant (12)

4. Wall (14)
5. Body (16)
6. Citizens (19)
7. Household (19)
8. Building (20)
9. Temple (21)
10. House (22)

The passage is rich in images, and these need to be considered individually.

E. REPETITIONS
1. Dead (1, 5)
2. Remember (11, 12, RSV)
3. Aliens (12, 19): 'There was a time, no longer'.

Note the balance between (i) Jew and Gentile, (ii) man with God, man in God.

F. KEY WORDS
1. Grace (5, 8)
2. Circumcised (11)
3. Covenant (12)
4. Law (15)
5. Reconcile (16)

G. CHARACTERS
(General not particular in 1, 2, 3)
1. Gentile (1–3, 11)
2. Jew (11, 12)
3. Christian (4–10, 13–22)
4. God (4–10)
5. Jesus (6, 7, 10, 13–18, 20–22)

H. QUESTIONS
Questions centre on the main theme, God's salvation.
1. From what are we saved? (1–3)
2. How is salvation achieved? (4–9)
3. How does it affect the community? (13, 15, 16, 18)

4. Is it a state already 'achieved', or does it imply growth? (21, 22)

5. To what end? (10, 21, 22)

Once the basic analysis has been done it is easier to return to the main theme and elucidate it more fully.

Further study—The theme of salvation in Paul's Epistles: trace key words (F.) through the Bible.

Conclusion

Three passages of varying kinds—poetry, narrative and reasoned argument—have been included for analysis to try to show in practice how the method suggested can be applied. No method is fool-proof for the immense variety of writing found in Scripture, but it is hoped that these suggestions will help the reader to make a start, digging for himself to find the enormous wealth of material in the Bible.

4 Character and Background Study
PAMELA WHITE

The word 'character' is Greek. In its classical usage it meant 'an impress', 'a distinctive mark', and then 'likeness'. This has its significance when we come to study biblical characters, for it encourages us to look for the impress of Another's hand on them, the distinctive mark or marks which God has made on their whole being. In studying a biblical character we are seeing above all God's impress upon him, a unique individual placed by Him in a particular environment among particular people.

As Christians we too are being refashioned by God. Paul tells us that 'we are his workmanship' (Eph. 2:10), newly created in Christ Jesus whose character we should increasingly bear. Any study of biblical characters, of God's methods of moulding His children and their response, has practical implications for us. The value of such study is that our sympathy engages with the individuals as they act or fail to act in their situations. So we are more alert to appreciate what God was teaching them, how He was rebuking or encouraging them, and how consistently He dealt with them.

Because He is the same God we can relate our experience to theirs, and can start to see with them what He is teaching about Himself and His will. The New Testament gives us instances of the value of character-study. James, for example, remarks that Elijah is an illustration of the potential effectiveness of prayer: though he was only 'of like nature with ourselves' his prayers resulted in events of significance to the whole course of Israel's history (Jas. 5:16–18). Similarly, the writer of the letter to the

Hebrews demonstrates not by argument but by illustration the power of faith. He refers to many Old Testament figures whose lives, as the readers would find if they studied them, had been characterized by an exemplary dynamic faith (Heb. 11).

The biblical characters we study are not only examples to us of how we should 'run with perseverance the race that is set before us'; they were also historical individuals, actors in the unfolding drama of God's redemption. We should therefore try to discover something of an individual's background and environment before we study what he learned of God and what kind of example he is setting us.

Choosing a character

Suitable starting-points are New Testament references to Old Testament characters (*e.g.* Heb. 11; Gal. 3:7; Lk. 4:27), or merely characters encountered in daily Bible-reading.

Background

Once a character has been selected for study, it is worth asking certain questions. Who wrote what we know about him? What is the date of writing, and how long before then did the individual live? Where did he live? What was everyday life like in his time? What about the state of international politics and of religion?[1] Answers to these questions 'fix' an individual, and prevent fanciful spiritualizing of what he said and did.[2]

Sifting the material

Some biblical characters, such as Ezekiel (the subject of the study which follows), are both author and subject of the books bearing

[1] Books such as R. K. Harrison, *Old Testament Times* (Inter-Varsity Press, 1972); M. C. Tenney, *New Testament Times* (Inter-Varsity Press, 1965), supply useful information and pictures.

[2] John Hercus demonstrates precisely the value of this sort of background work for the light it can throw on characters, such as Nebuchadnezzar, Isaiah, or David, in his 'Case-books': *Pages from God's Case-book* (Inter-Varsity Press, 1962); *More Pages from God's Case-book* (Inter-Varsity Press, 1965); *David* (Inter-Varsity Press, 1967).

their names, but most are introduced in the course of a narrative of events. The relevant material has to be sorted out. Is it entirely biographical (or autobiographical), or is there a great deal of other material (*e.g.* prophetic) interspersed with it?

Preliminary read-through

Whether the material is plentiful or sparse, concisely biographical or prophetically discursive, it is helpful to begin by reading it all at a sitting, perhaps in an unfamiliar translation. This is the only way of making a fresh preliminary acquaintance of the individual, and of seeing him or her in context.

Detailed study

After the first read-through we can turn to study the material in sections. Taking one or two chapters we can study the order of events and the part our individual played in them. How did he emerge as a character? Did he honour God or let Him down? Have we really understood the way he must have felt as a middle-easterner, and in most cases a Jew? What were his aims and motives? How did he treat the people with whom he was in contact? How did he respond to their treatment of him? In the case of autobiography, what does he himself teach us about the lessons he learned (or wanted to teach) about God and man? What can we see of the impression of God's nature upon his personality? What in general terms can we learn of the manner of God's dealings with individuals, of His intentions for them, of His own nature?

Application

Then, lastly, we can seek to apply to ourselves the points which emerge. We are inevitably different from those about whom we read; our circumstances are probably totally unlike theirs; and yet we, like them, are human beings, children of a Father who never changes and who always treats His children consistently. What He did – and wants to do—, what He showed—and wants

to show—of His glorious nature, that is of supreme importance.
It is to discovering this that our study of the individual and his
response should lead.

An example: Ezekiel

Background

Some basic data in answer to the initial questions can be found
from articles and books on Ezekiel.[3] Ezekiel himself was almost
certainly the author of the book which bears his name. (For a
discussion of the question of the unity and authorship of the
book, see pages 13–20 of Taylor's commentary.) Thus we are
dealing with autobiographical material of a certain sort.

References to dates are, more than with most of the prophets,
regular and explicit throughout the book, showing that the years
which are covered are 593/592 to 571/570 BC. (See Ezekiel
1:2 and 29:17, for example.) Ezekiel himself was, it seems,
thirty years old when he began to prophesy (1:1 is probably
a reference to his age), and he prophesied until he was fifty-two.
There is no record of his death, nor of how long before his
death his prophecies were written down; but he most probably
wrote shortly before he died.

The question of Ezekiel's location has received unexpectedly
complicated answers. Basically and simply he was in exile in
Babylonia, living in a Jewish settlement in Tel-Abib by an
irrigation canal called the 'river' Chebar.[4] But because Ezekiel
addresses some of his prophecies to Jerusalem and its people
almost as if he were there, some commentators have suggested
that he was there for a time after he had been deported to Babylonia. Taylor and Ellison both set out the reasons why this is un-
likely, and for our purposes we can assume he remained in
Babylonia.

Babylon at the beginning of the sixth century BC was in
control of Assyria, Egypt and Judah. King Nebuchadnezzar had

[3] *E.g.* in J. D. Douglas (ed.), *The New Bible Dictionary* (Inter-Varsity Press,
1962), pages 406ff.; H. L. Ellison, *Ezekiel: The Man and His Message* (Paternoster Press, 1965); J. B. Taylor, *Ezekiel* (Tyndale Press, 1969).

[4] See J. B. Taylor, *Ezekiel*, pages 21f., for a description of this, and the map
on page 122 in *The New Bible Dictionary*.

first gained control of Jerusalem in 598/597 BC, and from there had removed to Babylon all people of standing and ability. These Jews were not treated as captives, but were allowed to settle in communities and contribute their skills as the Babylonians wished.[5] In its bare fundamentals life in the Euphrates valley would not have been so very different from life in Jerusalem (apart from there being a greater abundance of water, a rare commodity in Jerusalem)—mud-brick white-washed houses; simple clothes; a plain diet mostly of cereal and fruit; some horticulture; weaving; a little letter writing! But the Jews were miles from the Temple of God, and so their worship had very little heart (*cf.* Ps. 137). Furthermore, they were having to work for the heathen Babylonians, perhaps in large gangs digging the canal.

For Ezekiel to come to life, he must be seen against this background of foreign residence, and of the confusion and distress which characterized the exiles who had to try to live normally hundreds of miles from home (and from God too, they were tempted to think), waiting all the time to hear news of Jerusalem. He himself must have been 'upper crust' to have been in the first deportation, and, as a trainee priest himself, it seems likely that he was of a distinguished priestly family. Nothing about his new sphere of life can have been congenial to this young man. It will be interesting therefore to see with what character he emerged from it all.

Sifting the material

When we turn to a study of the man, we find that we have a book of forty-eight chapters named after Ezekiel, but no other references to him outside it. It becomes immediately clear that we have little written *about* him, but are presented with a large body of material whose content is visionary and prophetic. This ought not to be omitted, because it is through what he saw and wrote that Ezekiel has made himself known to us.

[5] John Taylor describes succinctly their probable manner of life (*op. cit.* p. 22), and there are photographs of archaeological remains from this Exilic period in D. J. Wiseman, *Illustrations from Biblical Archaeology* (Tyndale Press, 1958).

Preliminary read-through

It may seem a tall order with the book of Ezekiel, but to read it through at a sitting is an extraordinary experience. The first chapter is the record of an exalted but very complicated vision, and as the chapters proceed we follow Ezekiel through other visionary experiences, through long periods of acting out his message, through terrifying denunciations of Jerusalem and many nations, and through personal loneliness and tragedy, to a triumphant hope for the future. He appears a gaunt, splendid, lonely figure, totally in the hands of God, almost as strange to his contemporaries as he is to us. Many have tried to categorize and diagnose his strangeness. The attempt is unprofitable, for whatever his psychological state might have been, he gave a devastating message whose significance was as clear as the media for receiving and conveying it were unusual.

Detailed study

Space precludes a full examination of the book, so what follows is in the nature of a short summary. He was twenty-five years old when he was carried off to Babylon. This must have represented a terrible blow to him, as he would probably have been in the middle of his long and detailed training as a priest. But in the year in which he should have become a priest back home in Jerusalem, God called him to a job even more vital and crucial than that for which he had been training. Ezekiel had to be a 'watchman' (chapters 3, 33). This meant warning the exiled Jews of the imminent fall of Jerusalem, and assuring them that it was precisely *because* God was faithful to His covenant that this had to happen, since His people had rejected Him. It meant also looking on to the future when God would search out His people as a shepherd looks for lost sheep (chapter 34), and restore them as a revived nation (chapter 37) to their own land (chapter 36).

To get this across, Ezekiel spent days 'acting strangely' (chapters 4, 5, 12, 24). Only thus, and through periods of grim silence, could he bring the exiles to *think*. Sometimes God gave him a verbal message, and then he shattered all his hearers' illusions as he built up a picture of sin and consequent destruction in all those nations, primarily Judah, who had turned against

God. Throughout he was unselfconscious to a remarkable degree. Only occasionally do we see Ezekiel's self coming across; the *priest* who baulked at the use of human dung for a fire, and was allowed to use cattle dung instead (4:12ff.); the *loving husband* whose grim control held back his tears at the death of 'the delight of (his) eyes' (24:15ff.); the *human being* who felt 'bitter' and 'overwhelmed' (3:14f.) at the magnitude of the responsibility of being God's watchman amongst an unresponsive people.

For most of the time Ezekiel was held at arm's length by his fellow-exiles, and in the light of this loneliness the courage of his denunciations is amazing. His language, too, is powerful, devastating, sometimes coarse. But that is not the whole story. Sometimes his advice was sought (20:1), and when he was shown to have been right about the fall of Jerusalem, he was on his way to becoming the idol of fashion (33:30–33). On the other hand, the warmth of his vision of the future is tender and calm. And it is to Ezekiel, with Jeremiah, that we are indebted for the grandeur of the concept that each individual is responsible as an individual to God (chapter 18); that God has 'no pleasure in the death of the wicked, but that the wicked turn from his way and live' (33:11); and that God, in response to His people's need, says 'I, I myself will search for my sheep.... I myself will be the shepherd of my sheep' (34:11, 15).

The last eight chapters of the book are dignified and bright, as the orderly, priestly mind of Ezekiel sees in vision how the Temple and land will be restored. Lovingly and patiently he works over all the details with his heavenly guide, the agony of the departure of God's glory from the Temple (chapter 10) forgotten now as he hears the restored city's new name, 'The Lord is there' (48:35).

Application

The Lord, His presence (not localized in Jerusalem), and the implications of that presence, are what make Ezekiel the man he is. To his extraordinarily sensitive inner eye come visions of the glory of the Lord such as none was to see save the author of the Apocalypse; on his keen conscience dawn the implications of the Jews' rejection of the divine presence; through his totally committed life come messages of warning and hope, conveyed with a self-abandonment, and an integrity of purpose which show up our allegiance to God for the tawdry thing it is. His God meant business. So therefore did he.

And Ezekiel knew his God was with him. The presence of God with His people is something which we tend to take for granted. Ezekiel was far more appreciative of the wonder of it: he had feared that absence from Jerusalem meant absence from God, but God had met him there in exile in a splendour as glorious as a mere man could comprehend. And God meets us, now, wherever we are. His assurance of His presence is made to us through Jesus, Himself, who as Immanuel, God with us, has promised to be with us 'always, to the close of the age'. To this presence we should respond in obedience and confident faith, as Ezekiel did.

Ezekiel is an exciting figure. This has been but a bare introduction to him, as the reader will find when he comes to study his book for himself. The God who created the man thus uniquely, who set him in those strange surroundings, and who moulded all his gifts and temperament into an integrated whole, is our God, and is dealing just as purposefully with us.

Further study

The reader might find it helpful to extract the suggestions and questions from this chapter and use them as a guide to further character study. Ezekiel himself would provide a suitable starting-point, as there is much more to add to what has been included in this outline. Working with the same list of questions further extended studies could be made (*e.g.* of each of the patriarchs, or the first kings, or Jeremiah), or much shorter studies (*e.g.* of Ruth, Elijah, Ezra, Hosea, Amos, or Jonah). Among New Testament characters, Peter, John, Mark, Barnabas, Andrew and Paul are some about whom there is material which can be collected and studied in the same way. A disciplined approach, in trying to answer all the questions, will bring with it the excitement of discoveries as varied as the characters themselves.

5 Word Study
DICK FRANCE

The Bible is the Word of God, and its words convey the revelation of God. It is natural, then, that we should expect to learn from God by studying the *words* of the Bible, and it is such study, particularly the separate study of individual words, which is the theme of this chapter.

Now it is obvious that a single word by itself conveys very little. Simply to pronounce the word 'holy' may suggest many different things to different people, but it will certainly not convey the full biblical idea of holiness. For that, we must study the word *in its various contexts*, going through the biblical uses of 'holy' and 'holiness' one by one to discover from each passage where they are used just what the word is meant to convey. Thus we shall gradually build up a picture of holiness as the Bible understands it. But even that is not the end of our study, for the aim is not simply theological understanding. As we understand what is meant by the holiness of God, we shall find ourselves, if our study is more than an academic exercise, loving and fearing God in a new way, as the men who wrote the books of the Bible loved and feared Him; and we shall begin to perceive what a staggering demand He makes, 'You shall be holy; for I the Lord your God am holy' (Lv. 19:2). The result will be not only a new understanding of holiness, but a new desire and a new experience of it. That is the ideal.

In other words, the word study we are concerned with in this chapter is not lexicography. It may begin there; but our ultimate aim is not to study linguistics, but revelation, not to learn

Hebrew or Greek, but to learn the mind of God and to respond to His word.

Problems

So far, this sounds fine. But there are problems which make valuable word study a hazardous business. Two main cautions need to be given at the outset.

1. A single word is seldom an adequate guide to a biblical idea

In a few cases, it is true, the study of the uses of a single word will give a fairly comprehensive picture of the idea concerned. Some examples might be 'ark', 'lot', 'priest', 'baptism'. To go through all the uses of one of these words will yield a fairly complete survey of the biblical teaching on that theme; word and theme correspond fairly exactly. But that is because these are all relatively restricted, sharply defined ideas. When we turn to the major theological ideas of the Bible, there is no such close correspondence between word and theme. For instance, the phrase 'the living God' is used just fifteen times in each Testament, but it would be ludicrous to suggest that the idea of the 'livingness' of God is restricted to these passages: it has been regarded, not unjustly, as the key to the whole biblical doctrine of God. Again, the word 'hell' does not occur frequently, but the idea is clearly present, in many different verbal forms, throughout the New Testament.

What this means for our purpose is that it is 'theme study' (see the next chapter) which is our ultimate aim, and word study is only valuable as a means to pursuing a given theme. Sometimes it is a fairly effective means, but often it is completely inadequate. We must not imagine that when we have looked up in our concordance all the uses of 'create', or 'heaven', or 'coming', we have discovered all that the Bible has to say about the work of God in creation, or about the believer's destiny, or about the return of Christ. We have barely scratched the surface.

We must, then, be aware of this limitation. It does not invalidate word study altogether, as we hope to show, but it does indicate that it must always be a means to an end, that end being 'theme study'. We are interested in ideas, not words, and there are few ideas which are entirely tied to a single word.

2. The Bible was not written in English (not even the English of 1611!)

This involves us in a serious problem for word study. Assuming that we have not learned the sacred tongues, we must rely on translations, and no translation is perfect, because no two languages correspond exactly. On the one hand, some words used in the English Bible represent two or more quite different words in the original, and to lump them together may lead to serious misunderstanding. For instance, it is well known that the English verb 'love' translates two Greek verbs, *phileō*, which refers to friendship and affection, a matter largely of the emotions, and *agapaō*, which refers to the very practical and demanding phenomenon of 'Christian love'. The alternation of these two verbs in John 21:15–17 is seen as deeply significant by most commentators, but the distinction is lost in most of the English versions, and therefore in the concordances as well. Other examples include 'know', translating Greek *oida* and *ginōskō* (roughly the equivalents of French *savoir* and *connaître*); 'power', translating Greek *dynamis* (strength) and *exousia* (authority); 'man', translating Hebrew *'ādām*, Greek *anthrōpos* (human being) and Hebrew *'îš*, Greek *anēr* (a particular male, even 'husband').

But on the other hand, even if there were one English word to each Hebrew and Greek word, our troubles would be only just beginning, for it is very seldom that the range of meanings in one English word would do justice to the complexity of the original. A word study of 'word', for instance, must reckon with the fact that the AV translates Hebrew *dābār* as 'word' 770 times, 'thing' 215 times, 'matter' 63 times, and has well over fifty other words and phrases to try to convey the nuances of the meaning of *dābār*. On a more clearly 'theological' level, Hebrew *ṣedāqā*, which the AV tries valiantly to confine within the straitjacket of 'justice' and 'righteousness', is now agreed to mean as frequently 'vindication' or 'deliverance', and is so translated often by RSV

and others. (Compare, for example, the AV and RSV translations
of Isaiah 51:5–8.) As for Hebrew *ḥeseḏ*, one of the richest words
in the Hebrew Old Testament, it has long been regarded as un-
translatable into English. The AV tried 'mercy', 'goodness',
'kindness', 'loving-kindness' and many others; RSV gets nearer
with 'steadfast love'; but I defy anyone to produce an English
equivalent which will always do justice to *ḥeseḏ*. How do you do
a word study on a word like that in English? Nor is the case
much better in the New Testament. *Psyche* is sometimes translated 'life', sometimes 'soul', while *parakaleō* appears variously as
'beseech', 'comfort', 'exhort' and others. Unless you have very
great faith in your translator's judgment, you are at a serious
disadvantage when you have to work in English.

And even if we had an exact English 'equivalent' to each
Hebrew and Greek word, it is seldom that it would be *really*
equivalent. The words in any language reflect the thoughts of
those who speak that language. The Hebrews, the Greeks and
the English not only use different languages, but they think
different thoughts. If this were not so, there would be no need
for word study at all: to say the English word would be to
convey the whole range of meaning of the Hebrew or Greek
equivalent, and there would be no need to trace it through all its
uses to determine what it really conveys. But in fact this *is*
necessary, and it is here that word study, which is really an
attempt to get inside the skin of the Hebrew or Greek authors,
proves its value. But this very fact warns us of a danger, that we
may be, quite unconsciously, influenced by the peculiar connota-
tions of our English 'equivalent', which may be quite foreign to
what the Hebrew or Greek intends. There is, for instance, an inevitable note of uncertainty and wishful thinking in the English
word 'hope' which weakens the confident, joyful looking-forward
of the Greek *elpis*. And what Englishman can speak of 'mystery'
without thinking of something strange and obscure, which
must be puzzled out? But the Greek *mystērion* means a secret
which no man could unravel, but which God has plainly revealed
to His people.

This second caution then leads to two practical conclusions.
First, we must always allow the context to indicate the meaning

of the word being studied, whatever our English 'equivalent' might suggest. Second, our word study needs to be based not on the English words but on the Hebrew and Greek originals. The first sounds possible, though difficult; the second quite impossible. We go on to explore how far valuable word study *is* a practical possibility for those who are restricted to the English, and we do this by making a few practical suggestions, and by one very sketchy example of what may be achieved in this way.

Suggestions

1. Learn Hebrew and Greek

No, that is not meant to be facetious! For the Christian who is concerned to understand his Bible as accurately as he can, and who has at least a reasonable ability for learning languages, there could be few better uses of spare time. Lovers of the Bible compare rather unfavourably with lovers of Homer or Racine or Goethe in their willingness to take trouble to understand and appreciate what they read.

2. Use an analytical concordance

Failing the acquisition of the original languages, and even after it, most of the problems raised by the language question are solved by this invaluable tool. There are several such concordances, but the best-known and most useful is Robert Young's *Analytical Concordance to the Holy Bible*.[1] Based on the AV, it lists the occurrences of each English word under the various Hebrew and Greek words (transliterated) which that word translates. Then an appendix lists all the English words used in the AV for each Hebrew and Greek word. So, without knowing a word of Hebrew or Greek, it is possible, by using these two classifications, to trace the uses of any word of the original; and in the process you are likely to learn painlessly a significant smattering

[1] *Analytical Concordance to the Holy Bible* (Lutterworth, 8th ed. 1939). J. Strong, *The Exhaustive Concordance of the Bible* (Hodder and Stoughton, 1894) is another concordance (to both AV and RV) which makes it possible to discover the meaning behind words which, though identical in English, are different in the original.

of the more important Hebrew and Greek words and their theological implications.[2]

3. Compare different translations

This is often a useful way of getting at the real meaning of a word or phrase, as each translation is likely to bring out a different facet of its meaning, There are dangers here, however, in that many translations, notably the NEB, paraphrase rather freely, and their paraphrases may reflect rather the thought-forms and preferences of the translator(s) than those of the original. The *Amplified Bible*, with its rather cumbersome lists of possible translations for a word, intended to bring out the range of meaning of the original, may well be helpful here. But a word study of the sort we are considering will give a clearer picture of a word's significance than any translation or range of translations, and will enable you to produce your own 'perfect' version!

4. In studying a New Testament word, do not forget the Old Testament

Probably all but one of the writers of the New Testament books were Jews, and the religion they preached was one founded squarely on the Old Testament. Scholars are pretty well agreed these days that, while classical and popular Greek may have some useful light to shed on the meaning of New Testament words, the chief source for understanding New Testament thought is the Old Testament. So do not study the New Testament use of a word in isolation; there are few significant words in the New Testament which are not considerably illuminated by delving into the Old Testament background to their meaning.

[2] There are no comparable concordances for other versions of the Bible. But Young's can quite easily be used in conjunction with other versions, provided that they are not too paraphrastic and that you have an AV at hand. The process of finding the Hebrew or Greek equivalent of a word merely involves using the AV as the index to the concordance. From then on the procedure is the same as above. *E.g.* to find other occurrences of the word for 'steadfast love' (Ps. 136), you have first to turn to the AV to find that it is there translated as 'mercy'. In the concordance the Hebrew original is given as *chesed*, and from there the study continues.

5. Choose your word carefully

There is little to be gained by a study of the use of 'if' and 'and' in the Bible. What words *are* likely to yield valuable material from such a study? Most obviously, the important theological words; you will hardly go unrewarded, both in doctrinal understanding and in devotional and practical guidance, from a study of 'holy', 'fear', 'love', 'law', 'repent', 'faith', 'grace', 'peace', or 'gospel', to name but a few, not to mention the more forbidding Latin-type words, 'propitiation', 'redemption', 'reconciliation', 'sanctification'. Few would dispute the value of such study, provided that the cautions made above are observed. Many can thank God for valuable lessons learned in this way.

It may sometimes be more profitable to study a phrase rather than a single word, and this is not difficult to do with a concordance. 'Walk with God', 'man of God', 'in Christ', 'day of the Lord' would be relatively easy and profitable phrases to trace. But apart from a few clearly defined phrases like these, the possibility of varying English translations is clearly greater for phrases than for single words, and so the task becomes more complicated.

So far we have dealt with words which clearly have a valuable message. But is there also a place for word study on more ordinary, everyday words, such as 'stone', 'fruit', 'dog', 'run', 'white'? This might seem to be a dead end, but in fact there is a possibility of useful word study even here, for such words, while they are often used in a purely mundane way, may also be used metaphorically, or as illustrations of spiritual truth, and a study of the uses of the word may throw much light on the point of the metaphor or illustration.

Take, for instance, the word 'rock'. There would not be much spiritual value in studying minutely every reference to rocks in the Bible. It is true, but it is not of any great theological significance, that a Midianite prince was killed on a rock (Jdg. 7:25), or that rocks are a refuge for badgers (Ps. 104:18). But when God is referred to as a 'rock', which He frequently is, then the word becomes important, and we want to find out what special significance the Hebrews attached to rocks to make them want to use such a strange name for God. A study of the Old Testament uses of 'rock', with this end in view, will prove not to be a

purely academic exercise, and has in fact yielded material for a
sermon for the present writer, which was of real value at least to
the preacher! The other words listed above would give similar
results, and the list could be extended indefinitely.

What we must make sure of here is that we read the words in
context, and that we study what the author intended to convey
by using that word in that context. It is all too easy to import
fanciful comparisons and allegories which would never have
occurred to the original writer. The fact that God is sometimes
described as a 'rock' does not mean that every reference to a rock
is a covert reference to God, *i.e.* that the Midianite prince was
sacrificed to God, or that the badgers take refuge in God. This
may sound ludicrous, but is it unknown for Moses' being hidden
'in a cleft of the rock' (Ex. 33:22) to be interpreted in terms of
the 'Rock of Ages cleft for me'? So do not let this sort of study
run away with you, especially if you are gifted with a devotion-
ally fertile imagination. Try to respect what the author intended
to say, and do not assume allegory or metaphor where he
obviously had no such idea. There are plenty of legitimate
metaphors in the Bible without creating dubious ones! Here, as
everywhere in word study, the context must decide the meaning.

But, valuable as study of such everyday words may sometimes
be, the main focus of word study must surely be on the great
theological and devotional words of the Bible, and here, no less
than in the case just discussed, we cannot stress too strongly the
importance of allowing each passage to speak for itself, so that
our conclusions are dictated by what the author intended to say,
not by previous understanding of what are often all too familiar
words, sometimes imbued by long evangelical tradition with a
meaning which is significantly different from the biblical perspective. In word study, as in all study of the Bible, always let
your context be your guide.

An example: 'Fellowship'

What is fellowship? The communal consumption of tea and
biscuits? A type of instructional meeting held on Saturday nights?
An organization of young people, men, wives, or 'senior citizens'

attached to a church? Two or three Christians unveiling their
intimate personal problems and joys to each other and to God?
These and many other answers could legitimately be given on the
authority of current Christian usage. But what does the New
Testament mean by it? (And here, incidentally, there is for once
no direct Old Testament background to be considered, though
parallels may certainly be drawn between the community of
God's people Israel and Christian fellowship.) So we turn to our
analytical concordance.

Under 'fellowship' we find one main word-group, *koinōnia*
(abstract noun), *koinōnos* (concrete noun, = 'sharer'), *koinōneō*
(verb). Turning to the index of Greek words, we find that *koinōnia* is variously translated in the AV as 'communication', 'communion', 'contribution', 'distribution', 'fellowship'; of which
'fellowship' is used twelve times, 'communion' four times, and
the rest once each. *Koinōnos* and *koinōneō* yield a similar range of
translations, though 'partaker' and 'partner' emerge as significant
additions. To do the job properly, we ought to look up each use
of the *koinōnia* group under each of the English equivalents
listed, but we would save some time and cover most of the relevant ground if we restricted ourselves to 'fellowship', 'communion', 'partaker' and 'partner'.

Space does not allow us to do the whole job here, but it will
not be long before we realize that *koinōnia* is not primarily something which you *do*, but denotes a state of affairs, represented at
the secular level by 'partnership'. It means 'sharing', 'belonging
together', 'togetherness'. For the Christian it means that those
who have become God's people by faith are thereby *joined* at the
deepest level. They may differ in almost every other way, but
essentially they are sharing in a common nature, like members of
one family. Moreover, they have *koinōnia* with Christ and with
God, as they walk in the light with Him. Our study will soon
make it clear that any idea of fellowship simply as a group or an
activity is woefully far from the New Testament idea.

But the New Testament is seldom purely theoretical, and
koinōnia is a case in point. As we study the context of each use of
this word-group, we will find to our surprise that *koinōnia* can be
a very mundane matter of *money*. Christian sharing is not only in

spirit but in pocket. Christian giving is the necessary corollary
of the new birth: as you come to share in a common faith and
life in Christ, everything else is shared too. In fact, it may be an
unexpected discovery that out of the 45 uses of the *koinōnia* word-
group in the New Testament, ten are explicitly concerned with
this material aspect of sharing (Rom. 12:13; 15:26, 27; 2 Cor.
8:4; 9:13; Gal. 6:6; Phil. 4:14, 15; 1 Tim. 6:18; Heb. 13:16),
while five others are in a context which makes it likely that this
aspect was in mind (Acts 2:42; Phil. 1:5, 7; Phm. 6; Heb. 10:33).

This is only a small part of what may be discovered by a
comparative study of the use of the *koinōnia* group in the New
Testament. You must do the rest for yourself! You can hardly
fail to gain a richer understanding of the all-embracing results of
your new birth in Christ, affecting not only your relationship with
God, Father, Son and Holy Spirit, but also with your fellow-
Christians, in matters as diverse as suffering, glory, money and
the gospel.

Sadly, this one example must suffice, but if the possibilities it
suggests excite you at all, you will find plenty of material for
similar studies in the various biblical words mentioned in this
chapter, and the list is far from exhaustive.

Conclusion

Enough has been said to indicate that the present writer believes
in word study as a means to discover more fully the mind of
God in the Scriptures. But it will only be of value if it is treated as
a means, not as an end in itself. If biblical word study becomes
mere linguistics or lexicography, it may be very interesting, but
it is of no great spiritual value. Our aim is to discover the
themes of biblical thinking, and word-study must be pursued only
as a means to this end. Often it is an effective means, properly
used. Sometimes, however, study of an individual word, particularly in English, may prove a positive hindrance to grasping a
total theme. That is why this chapter began with cautions, and it
may appropriately end in the same way. Bible study of any kind
too easily becomes an interesting academic exercise, and the
spiritual objective is forgotten. Word study is no less open to

this abuse than other methods, perhaps rather more so. It is no
'Open Sesame' to the treasures of Scripture. But, if used with
care and prayer, it can hardly fail to leave the user richer than
before.

6 Theme Study
PAUL MARSH

This book seeks to show the usefulness of various methods of Bible study, and deals with ways in which specific passages of Scripture and individual books, as well as words and themes, may be analysed and evaluated. Our normal Bible reading habits may encourage us to think more in terms of books and passages —almost all our Bible-reading schemes, and the various commentaries which are readily available, tend to make this the easiest method to follow. Every method has its value, but the person who extends his study to incorporate word and theme studies extends his grasp of Scripture immeasurably, and enables himself to view God's Word as a whole, and to apply it, not only to an understanding of doctrine, but to the issues of contemporary life.[1] Such a method ensures a balanced judgment which the application of any one particular passage might not achieve. For example, an understanding of the character of God based on an exposition of Romans 9 will be deficient compared with the overall presentation of the Bible with its outstanding passages in Hosea, Amos, Job, Isaiah, not to mention other New Testament insights provided by the teaching and parables of our Lord. Notice how Christ Himself tackled the theme of His own death and resurrection when reasoning with the two disciples on the

[1] Before reading this chapter it would help to be thoroughly conversant with the contents of the section on word study. There the foundation for much of what we will now consider has been laid. To investigate a theme one must study the meaning and use of words. Therefore, little or no progress will be made in theme study until the purpose and method of word study has been mastered.

road to Emmaus: 'And beginning with Moses and all the prophets, he interpreted to them in all the Scriptures the things concerning himself' (Lk. 24:27). Luke 24:44 shows that this was Jesus' regular method of instruction. Paul followed the same pattern (*cf.* Acts 17:2, 3). These are object lessons in theme study.

What is theme study?

A biblical theme can range from the use of mandrakes in Genesis to the subject of the hundred and forty-four thousand in the Book of Revelation! However, this chapter is not designed to study the obscure. 'Take the big texts of Scripture,' Dr E. F. Kevan used to advise young preachers. Similarly, as students of God's Word, we wish to deal primarily with the big subjects of the Bible. This selectivity is wise, for the great themes of Scripture will provide us with material of inexhaustible dimensions. For, as we have been reminded in the chapter on word study, our objective is not merely to gain an intellectual grasp of the Word of God, but to immerse ourselves in its content, being moulded by its message. While the former may be gained in a matter of years, the latter involves a lifetime.

Some themes may be summed up in one Bible word; in this case their study involves simply the principles discussed in the last chapter. Others embrace a variety of words or concepts. Take the word 'grace'; it provides both a word study and a theme study. As listed in Young's *Concordance* this word in the AV translates two related Hebrew words and one Greek word. A glance at the appendix lists at the back of Young's indicates that *ḥēn* (*chen* in Young's) has a fairly regular and consistent meaning, being normally translated 'grace' (38 times) or 'favour' (26 times), although it also appears as 'gracious', 'pleasant' and 'precious'. There is, of course, a family-likeness between these various senses. Many of the Old Testament passages are very important for the light they throw on the use of the term 'grace' (*charis*) in the New Testament. Young shows that the word is translated by a variety of words including, in addition to 'grace' and 'favour', 'benefit', 'liberality' or 'gift', 'pleasure' and 'thanks'.

Sanday and Headlam[2] reveal the immensity of the word when they list its meanings as 'attractiveness', 'kindly favour' (as being from a superior to an inferior), 'goodwill', 'unearned favour', 'a state of grace', 'kindly feeling'. To these may be added its use to express a monetary 'gift' (1 Cor. 16:3), and Paul's experience of it as a divine enduement of 'power' (2 Cor. 12:9), and still its shades of meaning are not exhausted! However, the theological implications of *charis* in many of its appearances mark the word out as itself the key concept for a theme study in the further sense that it shows God acting as a superior towards inferiors in granting us 'unearned favour' (Eph. 2:8), and in that it reveals a state of grace (Rom. 5:2). Grace, as 'unearned favour', finds its place as part of the great theme or doctrine of justification, and justification itself slots in as part of the still wider theme of salvation. An example of unearned favour and its relation to salvation is found in our Lord's parable recorded in Luke 7:41, 42. It has become obvious, then, that when thinking of theme studies, we must have some idea of the identity and classification of the great themes of Scripture.

Themes to study

Think of the Christian faith as an organism: the human body has arms, legs, feet, fingers, head, a heart and many more parts which combine to form an integrated unity. Bible themes can be understood in rather the same way. An arm on its own is interesting: its fingers and thumb, its arteries, veins, muscles and nerves all provide material for extensive study. But given just an arm, the purpose of the fingers and the source of the arteries remain an enigma until the body is seen and appreciated as a whole. So with theme study. Individual words, themes, doctrines have their own particular points of interest, but they attain their full significance only when seen as component parts of the body of Christian belief. The doctrine of sin, for example, is in itself revealing, instructive and supported by experience; but it is desperately depressing until seen alongside the doctrine of grace.

[2] W. Sanday and A. C. Headlam, *Romans* (International Critical Commentary, T. and T. Clark, 1905).

And both these themes take on added depth and significance when studied in the context of the doctrine of God. Understand who He really is, in what His character consists, and then consider again the blackness of human depravity and the inexpressible generosity of divine grace.

Our objective in tackling theme studies is gradually to piece together the body of Bible teaching, so that—however inadequately —we can comprehend the whole. This will be no technical exercise, but an experience in which the Bible student is himself vitally involved. As the theme of sin is studied, the objective facts relate to subjective experiences and I see myself as I really am.

What themes demand attention? Consider the following structure. We may commence, reasonably enough, with the theme of *God*: this will include His being and nature, His attributes and His names. Under this general theme comes the distinctively Christian teaching of the *Trinity*. Next think of the Bible's teaching about *man* and with this will be inevitably linked a study of *sin*. So you could begin to break down this section: the nature of man, his fall, depravity, original sin, the nature of sin itself, guilt, punishment. These lead you to the *person and work of Christ*. Although it is customary to bring His person and work under a single, general grouping, for the two are essentially linked, one may divide and subdivide these themes—His divinity, His sonship, His incarnation, His humanity, and so on. Any study of the work of Christ calls for a detailed analysis of the *atonement*. A concept such as this could lead you into the more general theme of salvation, with its associated ideas—grace, repentance, faith, forgiveness, justification, regeneration, conversion, adoption, assurance, sanctification. The *person of the Holy Spirit* demands treatment as a separate theme, and so does His *work*. One result of the Holy Spirit's work is the formation of the *church*—another theme which, although very much associated with the New Testament, will send you back to the Old again and again. Among other things you will want to discover the essential nature of the church, its ministry and sacraments. The church looks forward to a great day when human history will be wound up by the One who brought the world into being; the Bible has a great deal to say about *eschato-*

logy, or the *last things*. It includes the second coming of Christ, God's ultimate purpose for mankind, and the consummation of all things.

Such a brief résumé of biblical themes, formidable though it seems, is obviously deficient and leaves many gaps. However these can be filled out by any book of Christian doctrine. Our purpose here is to demonstrate the united character of the Word of God. It holds together with a consistency which in itself gives testimony to its divine *inspiration*. And that is one of the many themes which have remained unmentioned!

Theme relates to theme, not only in the subdivision of the major heads. The great doctrines themselves cannot remain in solitary isolation. To quote one example, regeneration is referred to under the major head of salvation. But in the biblical scheme of things, there would be no regeneration without the person and work of the Holy Spirit who is God's agent in bringing new life to man. Not only so, His work would be ineffective, and regeneration a non-starter, were it not for the person and work of Christ, and behind Him, the grace of God. You may find it useful to set out these great themes of the Bible on a large sheet of paper, listing under each heading its appropriate subdivisions. Then run connecting links between all the related ideas. You will find that no one concept remains in isolation.

There is, then, one body of doctrine and every part is necessary and functional. This functional aspect must be kept in the forefront of our thinking when studying God's Word. What He has to say is relevant to the life we live. If studying the theme of sanctification fails to affect the moral and spiritual quality of our life, or if it only leads us into battle with a fellow Christian in defence of sinless perfection, it has been a profitless exercise. A study of law and grace will help us to think constructively about an existentialist attitude to life, and help us to reason biblically when trying to evaluate the claims of relativism, permissiveness and similar philosophies. As for the doctrine of the *church*, it can lead into new and constructive thinking concerning ecumenicity and give guidance as to membership of the local church and our role within it. Paul's words to Timothy have a practical significance: 'All scripture is inspired by God and profitable for teaching, for correction, and for training in righteousness, that the man of God may be complete, equipped for every good work' (2 Tim. 3:16, 17).

Tools for the job

Everything written in chapter 5, *Word study*, about the biblical languages and about the use of Young's *Concordance* and different translations applies here.[3] Even a smattering of Hebrew and Greek, or merely the mastery of their alphabets, opens up new areas of source materials. Such knowledge does not give anyone the authority to pontificate concerning the meaning of the original text; but it does give access to other men's scholarship. Our aim should be to build up a compact set of tools for the purpose of a Bible analysis, to have a library but make it functional.

The Englishman's Hebrew and Chaldee Concordance of the Old Testament[4] lists under any Hebrew word every occurrence of it as it appears in the AV. *The Englishman's Greek Concordance of the New Testament*[5] does the same with the Greek. Hebrew and Greek words are transliterated into English characters. Girdlestone's *Synonyms of the Old Testament*[6] and *Synonyms of the New Testament* by Archbishop Trench[7] are also old books, but still useful and worth picking up from a second-hand bookstall. And of course Hebrew and Greek lexicons can be put to good use.

A book on biblical doctrines will be found of great assistance. While one can usually go straight to a concordance for direction in word study, the procedure for a theme study is not quite so simple. In studying the Trinity, for example, a concordance is useless as far as that particular word is concerned, for it does not appear in the Bible. On the other hand, some themes are so vast that it would be difficult to know where to start. Thus one would not find much help in studying the doctrine of man if one were to

[3] See pages 58ff.
[4] Edited by G. V. Wigram.
[5] Edited by G. V. Wigram (Bagster, 9th ed. 1903).
[6] R. B. Girdlestone (Nisbet, 1897 and Eerdmans, 1953).
[7] R. C. Trench (Macmillan, 1871 and Eerdmans, 1953).

look up every reference in Young's concordance under 'man'. The English word itself is listed nearly 3,000 times and translates about twenty different Hebrew and Greek words and phrases. Having looked up every verse one's knowledge of the biblical theme might not, in fact, have been greatly advanced, as the mass of largely irrelevant references would have been over-whelming. In such a situation as this the need for a book on biblical doctrines becomes apparent. A useful little handbook is *In Understanding be Men*.[2] Its coverage of themes is by no means exhaustive, but it is invaluable as a base from which to launch one's studies. It has a good general bibliography of more comprehensive works, and its index proves to be extremely helpful. After each section has been dealt with—and the themes are treated in the briefest possible way—a list of passages and references is provided. Such a book by no means eliminates the usefulness of a concordance, but it provides a selectivity and a structure which are valuable.

An example of theme study

Brief reference has already been made to a word study which covers a theme study—grace. That one word provided ample material through a full use of a concordance to give an under-standing of its significance in Scripture. We look therefore at another theme which embraces several English (as well as Hebrew and Greek) words in order to express its full meaning. In making such a study all the tools, concordance, handbook of doctrine and lexicons, may be brought into play. Take the theme for which grace is the remedy, the theme of *sin*. A full study would include such ideas as its origin, its essential character, its effect on man (his place as a fallen creature), on God (His judgment) and on the world (its subjection to 'futility'). And it would then be related to the theme of *grace*, its answer.

We will restrict ourselves here to the essential character or nature of sin. There is a variety of approaches; one is through the book on Christian doctrine, which has the advantage of helping

[8] T. C. Hammond, revised D. F. Wright, *In Understanding be Men* (Inter-Varsity Press, 1968).

you gain a general 'feel' of the word in its doctrinal setting. In seeing the subject's treatment in *In Understanding be Men*, the difference between sin taken as a word study and its treatment as a theme becomes apparent. Sin is seen in the context of the Bible's teaching on man. Its origin, nature and extent are explored. Its relationship to conscience, guilt and punishment is defined. Such a book analyses the theme and provides the reader with Bible references to look up. These, however, are purely illustrative in their choice. For more detailed study the concordance is an essential tool. Young's, in setting out analytically every word it lists, enables you to see quickly the various originals of the English words, along with their particular shades of meaning.

Sin occupies two full pages in it. Notice how many Hebrew and Greek words are represented and the different shades of meaning they express. From these it is possible to build up a comprehensive picture of the nature of sin. The various words set out are shown to mean guilt, failure, error, iniquity, trespass, transgression, to err, to go astray, miss the mark, and so on. Look up references given under these particular headings, and at the same time ask questions such as, 'What does guilt imply in relation to man and God?' 'What do "trespass" and "transgress" suggest about man and law?' 'What does to "miss the mark" indicate about an objective standard of right?' Working through the references helps to clarify what the Bible teaches about these issues, and answers other questions, such as, 'Is sin universal?' Romans 3:23 declares that *all* have missed the mark. An analysis of these references to sin points towards answers to some basic contemporary problems. For example, if sin, understood as 'missing the mark', 'transgression' and 'failure', indicates the existence of objective standards, what bearing does this have on anti-authoritarianism and the permissive society? Young's *Concordance* shows that sin and sin offering are often represented by the same word in the original. What does this suggest about sin and its remedy? Working down the list under 'sin, error, sin offering, *hamartiä*', you will come to 2 Corinthians 5:21, which points to an answer.

A theme study on sin involves more than looking it up in the concordance, however. Our language is full of synonyms and other words which are associated with sin. Compile a list. Some will already have been noted as possible translations of Hebrew and Greek words; others come from thinking around the subject, and will include rebellion, unrighteousness, perversion, wrong, evil, lust, fault, blame and many others. Mark 7:21, 22 provides good research material! Again, looking up references under these words will contribute to an increasing understanding of the nature of sin and will again raise fundamental questions about man, society and God. This thinking around a word for its synonyms and related ideas is an essential part of any theme study.

Having thought about words for sin and their implications, there is another direction in which to explore, that is, biblical events which demonstrate sin's origin, man's corruption and its power over men, and God's attitude to it. Often these cannot be located directly by means of a concordance; the word 'sin' may not be involved at all. Your general Bible reading and background knowledge (gained perhaps through systematic whole-Bible reading, *cf.* chapter 1) will enable you to fill in the picture here. What incidents record human corruption? Among the many is the account of Ahab and Jezebel's exploitation at Naboth's expense (1 Ki. 21). Analyse the passages in terms of what sin is like and what it does to people, both the guilty and the innocent. Study the power of sin demonstrated in the events of 2 Samuel 11 and 12. Is this a commentary on Proverbs 28:12? Do David's reactions have parallels in modern life? What does this teach us about the constitution of man and of sin? Are God's pronouncements on such situations (2 Sa. 12) relevant today?

To think round a subject in this way begins to draw out a picture of the biblical concept and its implications for the student. So any theme study will progress. The example above, of one aspect only of the theme of sin, has been severely selective. The scope is clearly enormous; but so is the benefit when the challenge is taken and the lessons acted upon.

The Bible is full of themes, and Jesus Christ has set us an example in this method of study and exposition. At least one man could say, 'I did not shrink from declaring to you the whole counsel of God' (Acts 20:27), and to his Corinthian friends, 'Be imitators of me, as I am of Christ'! It is worth the effort.

7 Root Study

JOHN JOB

There are various things that the term 'root study' could refer to. We begin by stating two that this chapter is not concerned with.

It is not about the derivation of words. Actually the etymology of biblical words is not usually of great value in discovering the meaning of the text. As far as Hebrew is concerned, it is often extremely precarious. But even if it could be established with certainty, it would still have limited relevance. For example, the word for covenant (Heb. *berît*) is generally thought to be etymologically unconnected with the word for create (*bārā'*). But this does not at all prove that there was no connection in the mind of the writer of Genesis. And conversely, the original meaning of a word soon becomes lost, so that we cannot be sure, when a particular word is used, that the writer was conscious of its derivation—any more than we should think it significant when we are reading a sentence with 'pen' in it that the word originally meant a feather.

Nor are we concerned with form-criticism. Form-criticism aims to determine by examination of the literary shape and pattern of a passage what is its likely context in the situation where it was first used. A classic example is the hymn in Philippians 2 which, supposing it is right to regard it as a fragment of early Christian praise, pushes the quest for the primitive tradition a stage further back than the letter in which it is embedded. In assessing the value of form-criticism it needs to be said that it is worth while in so far as it illuminates the text. Too often the tendency has been to regard Scripture not as a message from

God to man as it is, but as a kind of coal-mine from which crystals of early material must be sorted out from a mass of later slag. Or to put it another way, there is more to be said about the ceiling of the Sistine Chapel than how Michelangelo mixed his paints.

The kind of study with which we are concerned here is that of the debt which one passage of Scripture owes to another earlier one. The process by which the canon of the Old Testament developed is by no means perfectly understood. But what is clear and uncontroversial is that Scripture was an organic growth in the sense that later contributors to the tradition were heavily dependent on the earlier. It is hard for us, surrounded by a plethora of books, to imagine a situation in which a nation's literary tradition is a very narrow stream. But this was Israel's case. However important, therefore, the distinctively new character of a writer's contribution, he was inevitably bound to a considerable extent by the tradition with which both he and his readers were familiar. The former sacred writings provided, as it were, a vocabulary with which to express his new message.

The practical implications of this are clear. In order to understand what any writer is saying it is essential as far as possible to saturate oneself in the literature with which he was familiar. Of course, it would be absurd to suggest that the New Testament is unintelligible to one unschooled in the Old Testament. Because of the way in which Jesus recapitulated His people's history and experience, there is a sense (though this must be conceded only with caution) in which the New Testament is self-contained and self-explanatory. But when we come to interpret the New Testament in depth, its Old Testament roots are so continually apparent that we cannot fail to want to explore them. Nor is it simply a question of finding the roots of the New Testament in the Old. As we shall see, later passages in the Old Testament have their roots in earlier passages. Passages in the Acts of the Apostles have their roots in the Gospels.

We have noted in the chapter on the unity of the Bible that the relationship between Old and New Testament can be expressed in a variety of ways. Each of the categories there suggested can be turned into a question when we approach a passage from the point of view of root study. Is there some Old Testament promise which is here being fulfilled? Is there some Old Testament disaster which is here being reversed? Is there some problem left in the Old Testament unresolved for which we have here the solution? Can we view this passage as the end of a story or a process begun in the Old Testament? Does it present the reality of which there are in the Old Testament foreshadowings or illustrations? Is this passage written in vocabulary the meaning of which is defined in the Old Testament?

The most obvious clues, of course, are direct quotations, and these can be picked up with the aid of a good reference Bible. In many New Testament passages, for example, it is claimed that some event in Jesus' life and ministry is the fulfilment of a particular portion of the Old Testament. Take the words, 'Out of Egypt have I called my son', which are cited in Matthew 2:15. Root study in such a case involves more than merely seeing that these words were originally written in the prophecy of Hosea. The question arises, 'What did they mean in their original context?' It is sometimes suggested that such quotations were torn from their context by the early Christians, and that no good is done by seeking light from the original passage. But this facile view fails to take account of two important facts. One is that Jesus Himself, according to our evidence, saw His work and His death and resurrection as the fulfilment of Scripture, and emphasized this very much in His teaching. It seems much more likely, therefore, that the Gospel-writers were following Jesus' own line of interpretation than that, on their own initiative, they treated the Old Testament as a kind of rag-bag from which to select isolated texts with no more than a verbal connection.

The other thing is that these direct quotations, frequent as they are, constitute only a small proportion of the references to the Old Testament. When the extent and complexity of the web of Old Testament allusion in the New begins to emerge, it becomes clear how fundamental the Scriptures were in the apostolic understanding of the Christian revelation.

What light then does the original context shed on Matthew 2:15? It is clear that there the word 'son' refers to the people of Israel, and the event recalled by Hosea is the Exodus. Yet

Matthew without apology equates the son with Jesus. Far then from being irrelevant, the original sense of the words points to Matthew's understanding of Jesus as the rebirth of Israel, a concept which is crucial for New Testament thought, because on it depends the view that the followers of Jesus are the true heirs of Abraham.

If root study consisted simply of tracing definite citations to their original context, it would still be a monumental undertaking. But, as we have said, this is only the proverbial tip of the iceberg. We need to add (1) passages which depend on a whole series of Old Testament passages, and (2) passages which, while having no verbal connection with an Old Testament passage, have a conceptual connection with one or more passages. These two areas are those which are covered in this book by the chapters on word study and theme study. A word study becomes a root study when the point of departure is its use in a particular passage of the New Testament (or a later passage in the Old Testament), and the object of the exercise is to elucidate the meaning of the word in the passage concerned.

Take, for example, the word 'salt'. A word study would discover a variety of usage. Salt was used to purify, to season sacrifices, to season ordinary food, and so on. But now suppose that we are doing a root study of Colossians 4:6. Then the question is which, if any, of the Old Testament passages where salt is mentioned throw light on Paul's injunction, 'Let your speech . . . be seasoned with salt.' Most New Testament commentators explain the word by the hellenistic usage of 'salt' (actually it is more Latin than Greek) to mean *wit*. But we need to ask ourselves whether Lightfoot[1] was not wiser to refer to the one and only Old Testament use of the word 'salt' in connection with speech in Job 6:6. There the point is that Job is rebuking his friends for their unhelpful diatribes, and he compares their effusions with the tasteless juice of a plant called purslane (in Arabic, purslane is called the idiot-plant for its froth!). If Paul had this passage in mind, then he is not saying that Christians should be marked out by their scintillating conversation, but that what they say should

[1] J. B. Lightfoot, *St. Paul's Epistles to the Colossians and to Philemon* (Macmillan, 1875), page 298.

be *helpful* to those whom they meet—exactly the opposite to Eliphaz and his friends' advice to Job. This fits excellently with the end of Colossians 4:6, 'Study how best to talk with each person you meet' (NEB).

Such an example shows how root study can be of vital importance in determining the writer's meaning, and not at all irrelevant pedantry. It also serves, with the simplicity of the biologist's amoeba, to illustrate the basic principles of root analysis, because in this instance, if it is right to see Job 6:6 as the clue to Paul's meaning in Colossians, there is only the one Old Testament 'root'.

But to show how the problem grows more complex, take a verse like Mark 14:24, 'This is my blood of the covenant.' Here is an apparently simple statement, but a moment's thought is enough to show that the term 'blood of the covenant' is scarcely intelligible apart from the way in which it is defined by the various Old Testament passages on which it depends. If we had to choose *one* passage, we should choose Exodus 24, where the blood of the covenant made at Sinai was sprinkled over the Israelites. But it is scarcely an exaggeration to say that the whole of the Old Testament (as that name implies, since 'testament' is simply the Latin equivalent of the word for covenant) in one way or another illuminates Christ's words in Mark 14:24. This example gives some idea of the scope of root study, though in such a case, it is usually possible to find a relatively small number of nodal passages. Here, for instance, one might think in addition to the Exodus passage of the covenant made with Abraham in Genesis 15, and the promise of a new covenant in Jeremiah 31.

The roots of a passage are not always biblical. Thus in the Old Testament, it is important to notice how the word 'covenant' is illuminated not only by such scriptural references as we have mentioned, but also by the archaeological discovery of suzerainty treaties of the late second millennium BC. And, to take a New Testament example, the Epistle to the Colossians cannot be fully understood without some knowledge of the terminology of the early gnosticism that was rife at Colossae—terminology which Paul 'de-gnosticized' to express main-line Christian truth: the word 'fullness', for instance, was used by the heretics to express the totality of the godhead to be approached through a hierarchy of innumerable angels. But Paul said, 'No. The fullness of the godhead was pleased to dwell in Jesus' (Col. 1:19). Appreciation of this use of his opponents' words highlights the point he is making—that Jesus is God made accessible to man; and not in the esoteric way by which the dubious philosophical or ascetic exercises of the Gnostics sought after Him, but in the simplicity of the gospel.

However, the extra-biblical roots of Scripture have received their fair share of attention in recent days and can be explored with the help of modern commentaries. It is our conviction, on the other hand, that it is particularly among the biblical roots of Scripture that there is much of value still unmined. And when one considers that it was precisely this approach to Scripture that Jesus taught His disciples, it is reasonable to claim that such study is a task not only for theological specialists but for all who call themselves Christians. Moreover, the only tool required, besides perhaps a notebook, is the Bible itself.

Up to this point, we have been considering passages which hark back to earlier books. Most important, as we have seen, are the references in the New Testament to passages in the Old Testament. But we must also pay attention to the way in which the prophets and psalms have their roots in the Pentateuch. Why did Elijah slay the prophets of Baal? Answer: 'The prophet who presumes to utter in my name what I have not commanded him or who speaks in the name of other gods—that prophet shall die' (Dt. 18:20, NEB). Why did Amos inveigh against those who lay down on garments taken in pledge? Answer: 'You shall not sleep in the cloak he has pledged' (Dt. 24:10–13, NEB). What did the psalmist mean when he said, 'I set out my morning sacrifice and watch for thee, O Lord' (Ps. 5:3, NEB)? Answer: his figure of speech was taken from the legislation in Leviticus 6:12, where we read, 'Every morning the priest shall have fresh wood burning on the altar, arrange the whole-offering on it, and on top burn the fat from the shared-offerings' (NEB). But again we must notice that the reminiscence of earlier books also takes place on a larger scale. For instance, in Isaiah 40–55, the whole theological argument involves understanding the return of the Jews from Baby-

lon as the re-enactment of the Exodus, of Abraham's pilgrimage
to the promised land, indeed of creation itself.

The roots of a passage, however, may not necessarily lie outside the same book in which it is found. Here, finally, are examples
from Genesis to illustrate the way in which roots may lie close at
hand. In Genesis 18:10 God, visiting Abraham in human form,
asks, 'Where is Sarah your wife?' This appearance of God with a
pointed question echoes what has been narrated earlier. For God
has said to Adam, 'Where are you?' and to Cain, 'Where is Abel
your brother?' These first two questions were the ominous
introduction of the God of judgment, about to expel Adam from
Paradise, and Cain from the arable land. But the third question, to
Abraham, is the gracious and condescending introduction of the
God of mercy, who is going to take the barren Sarah, Abraham's
despair for the future, and make her fruitful, so that in her off-
spring he may inherit the promised land of Canaan. Of course,
there is other evidence that the miraculous birth of Isaac is the
starting-point of God's redemption after the dark sketches of
man's degeneracy in Genesis 1–11. But in such details there are
important clues to the writer's purpose.

Again, in Genesis 7:13, we are told, '*On that very same day*,
Noah . . . entered the ark.' The phrase representing the italicized
words in the original is a highly distinctive expression (lit. 'in
the very bone of that day'). But in Genesis 17:23 it recurs, in the
context of Abraham's circumcision. It is hard to resist the
impression that the writer is saying, 'Do you remember how,
when God spoke to Noah, he acted *that very day* in obedience?
Now we see Abraham doing exactly the same thing. Noah
enters the safety and rest of the ark; Abraham enters the safety
and rest of the covenant.'

What practical steps may we take to equip ourselves for root
study? The first step is to obtain a good reference Bible. One of
the most reliable is the edition of the Revised Version which
contains full references. It is greatly to be hoped that the New
English Bible will eventually be published in such a way, but
meanwhile an added virtue of the RV is its faithfulness to the
shape of the original Hebrew and Greek texts, so that it is still
invaluable as a study Bible.

The second step is to extend the scope of the reference Bible by one's own additions. Careful reading of the Old Testament will bring New Testament passages to mind. Jot the reference in the margin in both places. As time goes by, some of these jottings will seem fanciful. But others will be corroborated by further evidence.

But the real secret of progress is the gradual widening and deepening of one's over-all knowledge of the Bible which comes from regular reading and study of it. For while much can be learned from retracing roots which somebody else has discovered, the only way in which 'new' roots can be unearthed is when a chord of memory is struck and the possibility explored that the writer of the passage which we are reading had the same thing stored up in his conscious or unconscious mind as what he wrote evokes from ours.

Examples

1. What promises of God are (a) directly (b) indirectly referred to in the first chapter of Luke's Gospel?
2. What disasters in the first eleven chapters of Genesis are alluded to in the following passages: Luke 23:43; John 10:14–15; Mark 1:9–10; Acts 2:8?
3. What problem is raised by Psalm 110:1? How often is it quoted in the New Testament? Analyse the way in which (a) Jesus and (b) the New Testament writers regarded their message as a solution for the problem.
4. What unfinished story does the writer to the Hebrews refer to in chapter 4? What does he consider to be the true end to that story? In the light of this, how may Matthew 11:28–30 be understood?
5. Consider Matthew 12:6, 41, 42. Compare Jesus' language here with that of Hebrews 10:1. How does knowledge of the Old Testament enrich one's understanding of these passages?
6. What message is implicit in the rending of the veil of the Temple at the time of Christ's death? How does the Old Testament invest that event with meaning?
7. Consider together the stories of Peter's escape from prison

(Acts 12:6ff.) and Paul and Silas's experience at Philippi (Acts 16:25ff.). What have they both in common with the account of Christ's resurrection, and with the escape of Samson from Gaza (Jdg. 16:3)? What other instances are there of similarities between what is recorded of Peter and what is recorded of Paul? What roots do such instances have in (a) the Gospels and (b) the Old Testament?

8. Take the account of Christ's temptations in Matthew 4. What is the original context of the three chapters from which Christ's quotations are culled, and how is it significant? Is it justifiable to see Exodus 16 and Psalm 2:8 as 'roots' of the Gospel-narrative? If so, what is their significance?

8 The Bible and Contemporary Issues
DONALD ENGLISH

Our reliance on the Bible encounters one of its most critical tests when we are faced with contemporary issues. The Bible is relevant—but how does it help me about drugs or abortion? One effect of trusting the Bible is that it changes our attitude to such problems. They cannot be regarded in purely relative terms, governed by convenience or situation. For a Christian they will often, though not always, become moral issues—and it is with such that this chapter is concerned.

The belief that the Bible, properly interpreted and applied, will provide the means of solving a particular problem underlies this chapter. Sometimes we will meet problems which are clearly and directly dealt with in the Bible, or we will find ourselves in situations where one of the specific injunctions (for example, in the Epistles, Gal. 5:16–24; Eph. 5:21–33; 6:1–9; Phil. 4:8–9; Col. 3:5–4:1) is applicable. In such cases it is the Christian's duty to obey without quibbling. Often, however, there are no unequivocal specific commands simply because the particular situation did not exist in the biblical era, and instead we have to follow the general principles concerning man's relationship with God and his fellow-man which are an integral part of the Bible's permanent relevance. Some of these principles are also to be found in the Epistles in places like Ephesians 5 with the threefold injunction to walk in 'love' (5:2), 'light' (5:8) and 'wisdom' (5:15). Some of the implications of those commands are worked out in the passage itself, but there are many more than that passage contains.

Some principles affecting behaviour

The only firm base for any principles will be found in God Himself, in His relationship with men and His intention for them. As the Christian models his life on Christ, so he will determine his moral principles in accordance with the nature of God. From this vast subject we might pick out the following aspects.

1. God's love

The Bible bears consistent witness to the fact that God is love, which finds its ultimate expression in the self-giving love of Christ (Dt. 7:6–8; Ho. 11:1–8; Rom. 5:6–11; 1 Jn. 4:7–21).

2. His righteousness

'... all his ways are justice. A God of faithfulness and without iniquity, just and right is he' (Dt. 32:4). From Abraham's recognition that the Judge of all the earth will do right (Gn. 18:25) to John's vision of the righteousness of God's judgments (Rev. 16:5), this theme runs through the Bible (*cf*. Rom. 3:21–26).

3. His holiness

God is perfect, so no imperfection can be attributed to Him. He is light; there is no darkness in Him at all. Nothing unclean or polluted can enter His presence; He is holy (Mt. 5:48; Jas. 1:17; 1 Jn. 1:5; Rev. 21:27; Lv. 11:44–45).

Consideration more specifically of God's *relationship to mankind* helps us define further our moral principles. God acting towards us asks for a response of receptivity and of co-operation with Him.

4. God is man's Creator

He made everything very good, and gave man a position of honour in His creation (Ps. 8:5–8; Gn. 1–2; Job 38–41; Ps. 148). Man is to make use of creation responsibly and to re-create himself.

5. He is man's Preserver

The biblical writers and our Lord Himself see God as intimately concerned in upholding His creation, and yet much more in keeping His children (Mt. 6:25–33). Again man is to share in this work.

6. He is man's Redeemer

As God redeemed Israel from Egypt at the first Passover (Ex. 12–13), so He redeems men of all nations from sin through Christ, the Perfect Lamb (Rev. 5:9). The necessity of redemption points to the fallen state of man and warns us not to look for idealistic solutions. It also reminds us of our constant duty to point men to God's offered redemption.

7. He is man's Judge

God's judgment of actions, words and thoughts, whether in the present or in the future, prevents us from assessing problems merely in situational or existential terms. At the judgment all men will be answerable for what they have done or have failed to do (Mt. 25:31–46).

Our principles are not complete however until we have also considered *what role God intended man to play in His world*. Man's creation and the early chapters of Genesis teach us much.

8. Man is a moral being

He has the ability to choose obedience or independence. His actions have real consequences and incur judgments (Gn. 2:15–3:24).

9. Man is steward of God's world

His authority over other creatures is the delegated authority of a steward (Gn. 1:28–30; 9:1–7). This is his co-operation with God the creator and preserver.

10. Men are dependent on each other

Cain's disavowal of responsibility for his brother is the antithesis of what God intended, as was his action (Gn. 4:9–11). 'You shall love your neighbour as yourself' perfectly focuses God's intention for man's social behaviour (Lv. 19:18).

The relevance of these principles to moral issues is clear. To apply them is not easy, but nonetheless important. How should we go about it?

Applying the principles

There is no simple 'right' procedure for examining a problem and applying biblical principles. It would be misleading to suggest there was. However something like the following steps, put forward for the sake of clarity, may be found helpful.

1. The first step is to clarify in detail what the problem is by gathering as much factual information as possible and by examining the arguments on all sides of the case.

2. When the nature of the problem has been identified and understood, decide what biblical principles apply.

3. Study passages of Scripture which seem to be relevant, thinking carefully about their application in relation to the changed circumstances of today.

4. If principles or applications seem to be in conflict check your interpretation of the passages involved. If they are still in conflict ask which is the higher principle.

5. Do not rely on your own understanding. Ask God to guide your thinking, particularly in distinguishing between your own preconceived ideas and the Bible's teaching, and test your findings with other Christians who are also trying to find out what Scripture teaches.

Seeking God's will and studying His Word never ends at the completion of study. Our conclusions need to be prayed about and acted on. When we hear God speaking clearly—and we must be sure that it is He—we are bound to be 'doers of the word' as well.

A particular case introduced: Abortion

Our approach to contemporary issues will be guided in detail by the nature of the particular one under study. When factual evidence has been gathered and initially assessed, then we can decide what principles are at stake. (It will probably be necessary to return to the facts once a general moral guideline is clear in order to consider its detailed application.) As the particular emphasis here is on Bible study we shall not attempt to assemble all the mass of facts available. But it must not therefore be thought that the first step is unimportant or dispensable: facts are God's and it is important in itself and for our witness that we take full account of them.

In considering abortion we have much information at hand as a background to the British 1967 Abortion Act,[1] and the questions which will need to be weighed up include the medical and social ones concerning the effect on the mother and the family, the status and sanctity of life, and whether we can differentiate between potential and developed personality. The advice and opinions of specialists in the fields affected (medical, psychological and social) and especially of Christian specialists will be of considerable help.[2]

With the facts in front of us we then turn to consider which of the principles are relevant. As the primary issue in abortion is the extinction and preservation of life, the principles which most obviously apply are that *God is Creator* and that He is *Preserver*. Life comes from Him and human life was the summit of His creation. Human nature shares aspects of divine nature (Gn. 1 and 2). Further God is committed to preserving life (Gn. 8:20–9:17) and once shared human nature Himself (Jn. 1:1–14). Indeed it would be hard to over-emphasize the value placed on human life in biblical thinking. We might take this as a primary principle, that human life is precious; as it is given by God, so it is to be taken away by Him (*cf.* Jb. 1:21).

Moreover, the principle that *God is love* adds depth to our concept of life as precious. He is not only responsible for it: He has an attitude towards it. For Christians this will make the problem of abortion much more than a purely clinical one. In addition the fact that *God is a righteous Judge* to whom we must give account will prevent us from seeing the matter only in

[1] *E.g. The Abortion Act 1967* (Pitman, 1969); *Supplement on Abortion to the Registrar General's Statistical Review of England and Wales: 1968, 1969* (HM SO).

[2] In this case the Christian Medical Fellowship has produced some useful material (*e.g.* D. M. Jackson, *The Sanctity of Life*, London, 1962). The fullest book on this subject is R. F. R. Gardner, *Abortion: The Personal Dilemma* (Paternoster, 1972), which has a good bibliography. Chapters 3 and 4 of V. Edmunds and C. G. Scorer, *Ethical Responsibility in Medicine* (Livingstone, 1967), are also relevant. J. N. D. Anderson, *Morality, Law and Grace* (Tyndale Press, 1972) deals briefly with this and wider issues.

terms of the human circumstances. We must add to this the fact that *man as a moral being* is responsible not only for his decisions but also for the results of actions dependent upon such decisions. The logical outcome of causing conception is the acceptance of responsibility for that life by those who conceived it.

Before jumping to the conclusion that abortion must therefore be wrong in every case, however, we must look more carefully at the character and activity of God, whose nature provides our guide-line. However desirable the preservation of all human life might be, God's people soon learned that in some situations it was not possible. Death received divine sanction as a punishment for certain offences at law, or as the result of the conquest of land promised by God to His people (*e.g.* Dt. 13; Jos. 6). Moreover, however universal God's love is seen to be, a high degree of selectivity is also present all through the Bible story. The choice of Israel—for the ultimate benefit of all (Gn. 12:3; 17:4; Dt. 7:6–11)—is a case in point. In the setting of sinful human nature and imperfect situations choices have to be made which may not be ideal but which are necessary.

We may add at this point the principle that *man is the steward of God's world*. This stewardship involves co-operation, sometimes by 'interfering with nature'. Agriculture, medicine and industry provide many examples. The test of man's stewardship is how far it fulfils God's will for His creatures, whether or not it interferes with the source of nature. Moreover, our Lord's example in applying laws needs to be remembered here. He never abrogated or denied God's moral law because it contained at its heart God's love and concern for man. For this reason He constantly went to the central meaning of the laws and applied them with compassion and mercy (Mt. 22:37–40; 5:17–48; 9:10–13).

Our conclusions so far may be stated as follows. Human life is God-given and precious. The normative command, enshrining the sanctity of life, is 'You shall not kill'. In some cases, however, because someone's life is to be lost anyway, or because man's sinfulness has produced an impossible situation, or because considerations of divine love and mercy require that those already involved in life should be protected, exceptions to the normative rule have to be made. Man, as God's steward and guided by the principles of God's nature and will, should not fear to make such exceptions. Nevertheless he should have no illusions about the exceptions. They are the lesser of two evils, required in certain circumstances but not themselves normative.

One final point raised by our conclusions so far is the status of the foetus in relation to human life in the world. Some biblical passages, however figuratively, emphasize the significance of individual unborn children in the sight of God (Gn. 25:22–26; Ps. 139:13–18; Is. 49:1; Lk. 1:41–45). On the other hand a contrast between the death penalty for taking human life (Lv. 24:17) and the lesser penalty of a fine (Ex. 21:22ff.) for causing a miscarriage (albeit accidentally) suggests that the foetus is not regarded as equivalent to a life. (This is all the more significant by contrast with laws on the same offence among other ancient Near Eastern peoples.) If a choice has to be made between mother and unborn child what evidence there is seems to be on the side of the mother.

Guidance about abortion, then, on the basis of biblical evidence would seem to be as follows. The normative rule, emphasizing the sanctity of human life, stands against abortion. In some circumstances, however, the situation is such that someone's life will be lost, or will be so spoiled as to be as good as lost. In such cases we have to reach our decision by establishing the spirit behind our normative law and by asking whether an exception to the law would not better express the character of the law-giver, known to us in Scripture and in Christ, and better fulfil His will for those involved. The fact that it is an exception to the normative law, however, and the importance attached to the foetus in the small amount of relevant biblical material, together with the strong emphasis on accepting human responsibility for the result of human action, show that the teaching of the Bible is opposed to abortion on demand for the sake of convenience. The way of mercy is sometimes to help a person to accept responsibilities, however inconvenient.

At the risk of being over-dogmatic on such a delicate matter we conclude with a series of statements. Wherever no serious moral or medical complication is present the life of the unborn child should be preserved. The serious medical complication would be the threat to the life of the mother and in this case biblical evidence points to saving her life, by abortion if necessary. (Assessment of the threat to the mother's life is a medical, not a theological one.) The serious moral complication concerns the potential for a fully human life (God's purpose for all human beings) for those involved. In a case of rape, for example, it would seem obvious that abortion should be allowed if requested, since the sexual act was an involuntary one. It may be that on other grounds there would be reason for judging that to forbid abortion would be to commit mother or child or both to an in-human existence. It must be stated again that this is not the same as abortion for convenience. But the provision for a decision of mercy must be kept open and we must pray for those whose responsibility it is so to decide, that God's nature and will may be adequately reflected.

9 The Bible in a Personal Quandary
MONTAGU BARKER

There are two types of quandary. As long as we feel confident that we are on the right road, all is well (provided that we are not deluding ourselves). But a problem arises either when we are confronted with a choice of roads, or when no road forward at all appears. In other words there is the problem of decision and the problem of depression.

Decision

It may be the question of what to study at college, what job to train or apply for, or which girl to marry; it may concern buying a house, or a car. We all face decisions. And decisions may produce anxious uncertainty, especially where things are complicated by competition or disappointment. In the perplexity which arises, people naturally seek for guide-lines. We weigh up pros and cons. We look for signs and clues. In doubt of this sort, we feel the attraction of some stereotyped procedure or rule of thumb. Particularly in adolescence or at the onset of middle-age, the fact that we are facing new situations in which we have no previous experience to go on confronts us with problems of this kind.

Primitive society met this problem with oracles, omens, magic and superstition. While its priestly practitioners set out for the most part to please their clients, as when Croesus was carefully not told *whose* kingdom he would destroy if he crossed the river, such recourse to oracles illustrates the desire, found universally, for divine direction in times of decision.

In theory the Western world dismisses this as invalid and we find Freud rejecting all religion as a mark of immaturity and of the fear of standing alone. But in practice the ever-increasing fascination with the occult and astrology is demonstrated in the pages of women's magazines and the daily papers. Many, on the other hand, resolve the problem by attributing everything to chance and evacuating all meaning from the concept of decision.

Where, then, in this confusion must a Christian stand? He believes that there is purpose and meaning in life. He regards it as vital when faced with a difficulty to find a way through it which fits in with God's will.

The explicit promise of Proverbs 3:6, 'In all your ways acknowledge him, and he will make straight your paths' is more than an isolated text. It expresses an understanding of God's providential care which is a central theme in the Old Testament. When the psalmist said, 'Thy word is a lamp to my feet and a light to my path' (Ps. 119:105), he was not only declaring that obedience to God's commandments was itself an acid test to apply to prospective courses of action, but also that life is a road— a meaningful journey to a destination, and one of which God is in control.

The example of Jesus Christ

But for a fuller understanding of the way in which God's Word provides guidance, we need to look at the example of Jesus Himself (see Matthew 4:1–11). He stood at the threshold of His ministry. And there is a sense in which, as He went for the forty days into the wilderness, the shape of that ministry was still to be determined. What kind of a leader is He to be? Various models occur to Him: Satan's suggestions all have a scriptural flavour— that He should retread the steps of Moses, by giving people bread (as though Moses had produced the manna), or of Daniel by courting certain death (as though Daniel had braved the lions as a circus-trick), or of David by defeating the surrounding nations (as though David's victories were his own achievement). Against these suggestions, Jesus quotes three times from a passage in Deuteronomy. The chapters from which His answers are drawn deal with the lessons intended for (but, alas, un-

learned by) Israel in the nation's time of testing. Deuteronomy
8:3 teaches the true reason why God fed the Israelites on something other than ordinary food: namely that life had a spiritual
objective beyond the material necessities of survival. Deuteronomy 6:16 deals with the time when Moses himself shared in the
unbelief of Israel by striking the rock at Massah, thus putting
God to the test. To 'test' God means here to try to make Him do
what we want, to fit in with our plans. Deuteronomy 6:10–13
takes us to the foundation passage of the Hebrews' faith. Only
God is to be worshipped. The Roman emperors had literally
made themselves into gods. To follow in their footsteps would
for Jesus have been to do the same. To enthrone self is to enthrone Satan. In refusing these temptations, Jesus thus sets out
on a life which will inevitably lead to the cross. He has come not
to provide bread, but to be the bread of life. He will not come
down from the cross any more than He will leap down from the
temple pinnacle. He will reign not by the tyrannical techniques of
those who deify themselves, but with the self-emptying love of
the servant of all.

Thus we see that Jesus finds in the Exodus story the pattern
for His life. The way in which He handled the Old Testament has
implications for the way in which we should use the Bible in our
times of testing and decision.

Our use of the Bible

The first point to note is that there is no question for Jesus of
producing the slick proof-text. The more one examines the
context of the passages on which He relies in making His
decision, the more the few words which He quotes are seen to be
the mere handle by which He takes hold of the message of whole
chapters of Scripture—indeed of the Old Testament as a whole.
Here then is the crucial question for us to ask ourselves when we
are looking to some particular verse to justify a course of action:
'Am I being true to the context of this verse? Am I quoting it in
a way which is consistent with the over-all sweep of the Bible, in
the kind of way in which Jesus Himself would have quoted it?'

When Jesus was confronted with His time of testing, the
scriptural ammunition which He brought to the battle was not

hastily thrown together in the odd afternoon's acquaintance with
the passages He quoted. His knowledge of the Bible had been
stored up gradually over years of study, prayer and meditation.
So it should be with us. The biblical message needs to percolate
into the depth of our thinking and attitudes, so that it becomes a
part of us, and our real self is formed by it. The moment when
Satan said, 'Turn these stones into bread', was hardly the time
for Jesus to start doing the Bible study needed for His reply.

Similarly our resort to Scripture should not be reserved for when
we recognize that we are in a dilemma; rather, the dilemma will
test the depth of that regular, systematic study of the Bible which
such a book as this takes for granted. This surely is the approach
which is being recommended by the psalmist who says 'I have
laid up thy word in my heart, that I might not sin against thee'
(119:11), and by Paul, when he reminded Timothy, 'From early
childhood you have been familiar with the sacred writings,
which have power to make you wise and to lead you to salvation
through faith in Christ Jesus' (2 Tim. 3:15, NEB). For an example
of one who had learned to use the Scriptures in this way and to
apply them to the practical issues of life, one might look at the
Letter to the Hebrews, where the writer draws principles from
God's dealings with Old Testament characters (Heb. 11).

But the conviction (which we have seen to be both itself
scriptural and Christ-like) that the Bible is the Christian's key to
guidance can itself lead to abuse.

One problem we have already hinted at, in the emphasis
placed on the way in which Jesus' quotation of texts was strictly
in harmony with their context. What is often mistaken for
scriptural guidance is a passage with bare verbal associations
with a person's problem. Part of the trouble here is that men and
women renowned for their Christian exploits have recorded
their use of just this approach to the Bible in search of guidance.
'Did not God honour it?' we may well wonder. We are not
denying that God may accommodate Himself to His people's
weaknesses (as He did with Gideon) in this as in other respects.
But this is no reason for modelling ourselves on the weaknesses
of godly men. We should be imitators of them *as they are of
Christ*, and no further.

The danger of this wrong use of the Bible lies in the ease with which we may deceive ourselves. In any dilemma, we look for the definitive sign indicating with divine certainty which way we should go. But the verse that leaps out of the page as the answer to such a problem may all too often not be a comment by God at all on the situation, but simply our own confirmation of our subconscious preferences. And not only preferences, but sometimes equally our subconscious fears. We may well want to do something which is in fact God's will, and be discouraged by a verse of Scripture which is not a genuine divine warning, but simply the guise in which our unfounded misgivings dress themselves up. It has to be noted that in Jesus' temptation, Satan was quite capable of providing apparently scriptural support for his wrong suggestions.

Further, we may point out that the Bible does not encourage us to believe that we shall see bright green lights indicating the right way at all life's cross-roads. It is important to distinguish between God's promises that those who are biddable will *be* guided and a promise which nowhere appears in the Bible that they will *feel* guided. When Moses asked for a sign that God was really calling him to rescue the enslaved Israelites from Egypt, what he received was not the kind of sign he was asking for at all. It was simply a promise that he would know in retrospect: 'You shall all worship God here upon this mountain' (Ex. 3:12, NEB).

Depression

Depression may be looked upon as an extreme case of the kind of dilemma we have had in mind in the foregoing treatment of decision. For a while the psychiatrist may look for a variety of symptoms to confirm a clinical diagnosis of depression, an obvious and important factor is indecision. The depressed person cannot decide what to do, because no way forward seems possible or worth while.

The examples of men of faith
The first way in which the Bible may be of use in helping a Christian in this situation is with examples of men of accredited

faith who found themselves in this same predicament. The mere
fact that there are such examples is an encouragement. For it is a
temptation in depression to see it as itself a contradiction of one's
Christian profession, and in this way despair leads to even greater
despair.

A full-scale treatment of depression is to be found in the Book
of Job. But other important passages include the account of
Elijah's breakdown (1 Ki. 19) and such Psalms as 73 and 88. In
the New Testament one might point to the experience of Paul at
Corinth before hearing good news from Thessalonica (Acts
18:1–6; 1 Thes. 3:5). It is beyond the scope of this chapter to
explore this material in any detail. Instead, we must be content
with showing by a few illustrations the kind of way in which
God can use depression.

God may well use such an experience to rid us of some false
preconception. It is instructive in this respect to see how often
this is the case in Scripture. Elijah, for example, had clear-cut
ideas about what ought to have happened to Jezebel in a God-
governed world, and when, after the triumph of Carmel, she was
left securely in power, he felt let down. He was to learn that
God's point could be made in other ways than by the kind of
flame-throwing with which he had come to expect injustice to be
visited. Not the wind, earthquake, or fire, which surrounded the
original law-giving, was to be God's characteristic weapon in the
hand of His servants, but the apparently weak voice of the des-
pised prophet. We often need to be reconciled to a way forward
which strikes us as undignified, lacking in panache, self-effacing.
This was the issue for Jesus in Gethsemane, and for Paul as he
faced the implications of preaching a crucified Saviour. It is the
issue which confronts us in the very crisis of becoming a Christian
and constitutes a large element in many of our crises as believers.

Another lesson in the story of Elijah's breakdown is the way
in which food, sleep and rest had their place in his recovery,
before the basic problem as he viewed it was broached. In this
way we are reminded that there is often a physical factor tied in
with what appears to us as a spiritual problem. It is very hard to
recognize that one may be ill when one does not feel ill—only
desperate. It is important to be able to recognize the point where

we can no longer cope with the problem ourselves, and require the special help that is available. This may be the hospitality of Christian friends, or the advice of a minister, or the help of a psychiatrist. Morbid preoccupations, fear which paralyses, an inability to break out of circular sequences of anxious, futile thought, these are all signals that we should look for Elijah's angel in human form. For they indicate that there are other steps to be taken, as in his case, before the future can be squarely faced.

Sometimes a depressed Christian requires no encouragement to turn to his Bible for help, but indeed spends hours on end studying it. This may strike him as providing the only way of escape from his prison of depression and indecision, since understandably he expects God to show him the way forward through His Word. But the Bible encourages us to look beyond its pages in such a situation. It needs only a cursory examination of the Book of Job, to see that the dialogue Job had with his friends was all about biblical issues; references to other parts of Scripture are legion. But in God's speech, which serves as a dénouement for the book, there is a striking freedom from biblical argument. Job is taken to the book of nature. And the point of this is to show him the extent to which the world is taken care of beyond his ken. In this kind of panorama, the volatile, bewildered mind finds fixed stars by which to begin steering afresh. Or if it is the kind of depression which has no doubts about the ordered universe, which finds reason for despair only in the guilt-ridden self, then the Bible turns us to the sure facts of the new creation, to the day in history when Jesus died on the cross, and the day in history when the tomb was found empty. The elements of the sacrament are particularly to be valued at such a time—for they come as objective tangible guarantees of the certainty that is being doubted. Namely that Christ died *even for me*. Was it not the end of depression for the Emmaus disciples when they recognized Jesus *in the breaking of bread*?

But although it is possible to abuse the Bible both by becoming locked up in the book itself, and by succumbing to the temptation to read into particular verses what either whim or fear dictates, there are two reasons for which its message is particularly applicable in depression. There are first of all the individual

stories which tell again and again of God's deliverance in
seemingly hopeless situations. These are powerful assurances
that as the dark tunnel had an end for one after another of the
men of God in Scripture, so there will be an end to our dark
tunnel. And if it is objected that tragedy does not always end up
as happily as in the case of Joseph or Job, we see, secondly, the
whole Bible pivoting around the two stories in which the
tragedy had a *final* quality, and yet God's providence still
triumphed. One was the destruction of Jerusalem—the hub of
the Old Testament; the other was the cross of Christ—the hub
of the New.

There is no full answer to the question, 'Why this suffering, this
darkness?' But the city was rebuilt. Jesus was raised from the
dead. The Word of God says much about the darkness of despair.
But what it says is that there is a light which that darkness cannot
put out. To study the Bible in depression is to kindle the same
flame in a darkened mind. For it points to the Lord who is with
us in the valley of death's shadow, though we do not know it,
and who will in the end meet us beyond it.

Conclusion

The Bible then provides no instant remedy for depression nor
any easy answers for indecision. We mistake its purpose if we use
it in that way. Its purpose is to reveal God Himself to us and His
offered salvation in Jesus Christ. Of course it does not leave us
without advice for the Christian life, but it does not set out to
remove the element of struggle from Christian living. Paul,
steeped in the Bible though he was, had to fight all the way
(2 Tim. 4:7). But it was his study of the Scriptures which
convinced him of God's abounding grace, upon which was built
his confidence for decisions of life and in face of death. It is by
learning the lessons which God wants to teach us through His
creation and revelation, diligently studied, and by living in the
light of them, that we will experience for ourselves the fact that
in His faithfulness He does not change. Because of this, when we
pass through various trials, we shall be able to recognize in them
the love of our Father and 'count it all joy' (Jas. 1:2).

10 Problem Passages
FRANKLYN DULLEY

If we take seriously the claim that 'all Scripture is inspired by God and profitable for teaching' (2 Tim. 3:16), we must take equally seriously the fact that some passages of Scripture seem to many people to run contrary to common sense and decency. There appear to be contradictions both in matters of historical fact and in doctrinal teaching. Events are described that we are taught to believe are 'scientifically impossible'. Then the Bible's morality seems at times to be at odds with what our notions of ideal justice and mercy would require. We cannot simply brush these things aside with the excuse that 'St Paul had an off day when he wrote that'. For, if this were true of his remarks about women in 1 Corinthians 11, for example, there is no reason why it should not equally be true of what he has to say about love two chapters later.

Basic principles

Scripture teaches that the God who inspired it is the Creator of the universe, whose hand is plain in what He has created. Man is made in His image, and our understanding of ourselves and our world has to be seen in this context. What God says to man in Scripture about human nature and history and what man finds out for himself by the use of his God-given faculties cannot be inconsistent. Whatever the direction that the initiative comes from, from God or from man, truth is truth and all truth is God's truth. In accepting the authority of Scripture, therefore, we are committed to the belief that there cannot be any final conflict between what the Bible says and the truths of science, history or basic human morality. Either a solution can be found for them, or Scripture is not the Word of God.

On the other hand, though we are committed to search for a solution, we are not committed in advance to any particular type of solution to any particular problem. In principle the difficulty may have arisen in one of two ways. Either we have failed to understand what the Bible is really saying, or we are wrong in assuming that the present state of scientific, historical or moral understanding is final and not open to correction. We must beware equally of a naïve biblicism that worships a particular exposition of Scripture as God's last word to man and is not willing to have its insight deepened and corrected by the Holy Spirit, and also of an arrogant scientism that forgets that all man's insights and theories are open to correction and that to deny the reality of the supernatural because it cannot be fitted into a formula is to put arbitrary blinkers on the search for truth. The natural and social sciences may fairly claim the right to account for whatever may be described in their terms. They cannot claim that nothing exists beyond what can be so described, nor that theirs are the only terms in which a particular event can be analysed.

Inconsistent?

There are problems posed by the Bible, however, which are purely internal ones. These are due to apparent inconsistencies within it, between, for example, the different genealogies of our Lord given by Matthew and Luke, the ascription of Goliath's death to David in 1 Samuel 17 and to Elhanan in 2 Samuel 21, the 'Matthean exception' allowing divorce for unchastity (Mt. 5:32; 19:9) where Mark, Luke and Paul make no such concession, or the different teachings of Paul and James about faith and works.

In approaching these it is important to remember that the Bible was written against an alien cultural background and in foreign languages. To understand it we need to project ourselves into that culture and to grapple with the difficulties posed by translation from dead languages. This means making good use of modern translations, Bible dictionaries and commentaries whose authors are abreast of current scholarship and whose presuppositions do not rule out the integrity and inspiration of Scripture.[1]

Broadly, four common solutions to difficulties of this sort may be listed:

1. Words and phrases in Hebrew and Greek may have rather different meanings from their nearest English equivalent. In Hebrew, 'son of' may indicate not only strict physical sonship but also any genealogical connection (grandson, great-grandson, *etc.*) as well as connection by adoption or belonging to a wider kinship group. Apparent inconsistencies in family trees can therefore easily arise without any material disagreement being present.[2]

2. Writers do not normally bother to mention what is familiar to their readers and will be assumed without specific mention. It was common ground in first-century Judaism that a wife's adultery provided grounds for divorce—and indeed for execution (*cf.* Jn. 8:5). The original words of Jesus' reply to the question about divorce may have taken this for granted, and only Matthew makes this explicit. This does not altogether solve the problem, however, because the word in Matthew normally translated 'unchastity' is not that usually used for adultery and may mean something graver. Whatever interpretation is placed on his words, he plainly agreed with Mark, Luke and Paul in attributing to Jesus a stricter teaching than either the rigorists or the liberalizers among contemporary rabbis.

3. Diverse situations require diversity of emphasis. Paul glorifies faith above works in writing to the Galatians because they were falling prey to a legalism that insisted on rigorous adherence to the ceremonial laws of Judaism as well as faith in Christ. James was faced with a totally different problem, that of a

---

[1] *E.g. The New Bible Dictionary* (Inter-Varsity Press, 1962); *The New Bible Commentary Revised* (Inter-Varsity Press, 1970); and the series of commentaries on individual books (in progress), published by the Tyndale Press.

[2] See *The New Bible Dictionary*, under 'genealogy', pages 456–458.

false spirituality that could see no point in bothering about the trivialities of earthly behaviour and was a cloak to complacent worldliness. Here it was vital to insist that 'faith', as James' readers understood it, was not enough.

4. The text as we have it may be corrupt or unintelligible through copyists' errors. This is a possibility in any document that has passed down the ages in handwritten form. The text of Scripture has suffered much less in this way than other writings of comparable age, and the places where genuine obscurity exists are relatively few and unimportant. Conjectural emendation is a last resort, only attempted when all other remedies have failed, and then only when a plausible explanation can be given for the error (*e.g.* confusion of words similarly spelt). Nevertheless there are a few passages where this is a reasonable solution. The matter of Goliath's killer is one of them.[3]

Impossible?

Under this heading fall miracle stories and fulfilled prophecies that are too explicit to be mere guess-work. When these occur outside the Bible, in the lives of medieval saints, for example, we tend to ascribe them to pious fiction and the credulity of a bygone age. The question is, therefore, why should we not do the same with biblical miracles and prophecies?

There are two ways to approach this question. The first is to accept the common-sense presumption that the laws of nature are not broken and to seek some explanation of the story that does not involve this. Short of rejecting it totally as a fiction, there are several ways of doing so.

1. The first is to take into account the progress of knowledge. What was only explicable as a direct intervention of God when the event was observed may not need this explanation today. The plagues of Egypt, or at least some of them, may have been straightforward consequences of an abnormal Nile flood, predictable by the modern geographer though baffling to Pharaoh and his magicians. The event is no longer strictly miraculous, though it is still either a remarkable coincidence

[3] See *The New Bible Commentary Revised*, pages 318f.

or evidence of God's providential concern for the Israelites.

2. It may have been recognized as providential rather than miraculous at the time, but the writer's concern was not with scientific description and prediction but with seeing the event within the perspective of God's redemptive purposes. He thus writes of God as causing it without intending to deny that at a different level physical causes were also at work, *e.g.* the east wind that drove back the sea for Moses to cross.

3. Following from this, the language of the description often makes it hard to tell whether a naturalistic explanation is possible or not, *e.g.* of the meteorological phenomena of Joshua 10:12–14 or 2 Kings 20:8–11. In the former the difficulty is heightened by the fact that the description is taken apparently from an ancient heroic poem, the Book of Jashar, and the language may have been deliberately figurative (compare the prose account of Sisera's defeat with the poetic version of Jdg. 4 and 5).

4. There is always the possibility that the text is not intended to be taken as literal narrative. Parable had a long history before our Lord used it (*cf.* 2 Sa. 12). However, like emendation of the text, this should be a last resort, not a first one. To justify the supposition that a piece of prose narrative is not intended as historical description it is necessary to be able to produce a reasonably close literary parallel for, for instance, writing fables round historical figures such as Jonah or putting fictitious prophecies in the mouths of long-dead prophets by way of commentary on present events; and it is also necessary to produce a reasonable explanation of why the author should have chosen this somewhat devious method of writing.

The second approach is to recognize that we cannot and should not expect to find a naturalistic explanation for every miracle in the Bible. A key point in its teaching is that God has intervened in the world. His creative power is not limited to the bare act of setting it going. He also acts to set it right, and in doing so reveals a new dimension to His character. A God who can do nothing to change the world is neither its Lord nor its Saviour. Miracles are therefore to be expected, and particularly where we find them, at the turning-points of God's redemptive plan, especially the exodus and the earthly ministry of Christ and the first few years of the church.

Miracles, in the nature of things, cannot be foreseen or explained. But there is here a partial test of their genuineness: (a) whether they further God's pledged purpose of saving and sanctifying a people for Himself, and (b) whether they deepen and enrich man's understanding of who He is. It is on these grounds that we reject the sort of miracle story that is typical of the apocryphal gospels or medieval lives of the saints.

Immoral?

The defence of miracles in the Bible is thus closely bound up with the vindication of God's character as portrayed there. Much of what God actually commanded or at least approved seems repellent to many people today. If it was wrong to blast Dresden or Hiroshima out of existence, can it, they ask, have been right to do the same to Canaanite cities? And is it fair to visit the fathers' sins on unborn generations, to condone slavery and polygamy or, the ultimate stumbling-block, to torment the wicked in hell?

Most of what people take exception to is found in the Old Testament, but the reality of hell as a place of punishment is unequivocally taught by Christ (*e.g.* Mt. 5:21ff.; Mk. 9:43ff.), and in any case we cannot drive a wedge between the Old Testament and New Testament portraits of God without questioning Christ's own claim that the God of the Old Testament was His Father. Moreover, the Old Testament itself entitles us to ask, with Abraham, 'Shall not the Judge of all the earth do right?' (Gn. 18:25).

On the other hand, God's doing of right must be seen in relation to its historical context. God does not expect man to do what he is not capable of doing. His plan of salvation and revelation proceeds step by step, and His highest demands coincide with His richest gifts. The full Christian ethic of love comes only as the culmination of the process, because it cannot be achieved except in the power of the Holy Spirit which could be liberated only through Christ's suffering and resurrection. What went before is provisional. The Mosaic Law was never intended as God's last word to men, but rather to mould a community into which that last word could come and be understood. There was no way to preserve that community in Canaan uncorrupted by paganism without the extermination of the Canaanites. The need to maintain a national community of this kind no longer applies; neither therefore does the duty to preserve identity by the extermination of corrupting foes. Similarly slavery is tolerated even in the New Testament, because to destroy it as an institution was possible only by tearing society apart. Condemnation of slavery is implicit in its moral teaching, but so equally is condemnation of class hatred and revolutionary violence.

In considering passages that seem sub-Christian in their morality, we need therefore to ask ourselves:

1. Is this passage *intended* to set a moral standard? By no means every incident is meant to be taken as a model—not, for example, the story of Jephthah's daughter (Jdg. 11:29ff.). Disapproval is often implied rather than expressed, as here.

2. Is its teaching confirmed and restated with clearer interpretation elsewhere in the Bible? If so, the interpretation supplies the key to the intention of the original.

3. Is the historical context still the same today? If not, then the teaching may no longer be directly applicable (*e.g.* that on women's dress in 1 Cor. 11:2ff.), though there is normally an indirect lesson for us—on the proper relationship between the sexes, in this case.

4. What alternatives were open at the time of writing? The choice of the lesser of two evils often has to be made, even by the inspired writers of Scripture. The prayer with which Psalm 137 ends is barbarous, taken in itself. But when we remember that it was written in the misery, disillusion and degradation of exile by a man whose hopes of God's presence and protection had been tied to the physical existence of the Temple in Jerusalem, we may wonder how else he could have expressed the hope of God's name being eventually vindicated.

5. How far is our inability to accept what the Bible says a criticism of us and not of Scripture? Rejection of Christ's teaching about judgment and hell, for example, can stem from a

sentimental unwillingness to face the facts that to be human is to be responsible for what one does.[4]

Most problem passages in the Bible will yield to one or other of these approaches. Nevertheless it is too much to expect that all its difficulties can be explained away simply. The biblical writers themselves experienced them (2 Pet. 3:15ff.). Instant wisdom, like instant holiness, is not a gift that God commonly lavishes on His people. For most of us understanding comes only gradually, through the illumination of the Holy Spirit, and through willingness to wrestle humbly, honestly and prayerfully with the obscurities and meanwhile to live following and obeying what we can understand.

[4] Further light is thrown on this problem in F. D. Kidner, *Hard Sayings* (Inter-Varsity Press, 1972).

Postscript

In this book we have been concerned with a number of techniques of handling Scripture. Inevitably, the approach has been an academic one. Yet the aim is not the mastery of a body of knowledge in the way in which one might master Latin grammar or Euclidean geometry, but to hear a person speaking.

The Christian with his Bible is in danger of making one of two mistakes. He may on the one hand imagine that the unaided human intellect is capable of grasping its message. The New Testament provides us, in the scribes, with a salutary warning in this direction. For here were men whose knowledge of the Old Testament was in one sense unsurpassed. But it was a knowledge of the face of Scripture, not of its heart. It was a knowledge of detail undismayed by failure to grasp the overall sweep of the message. In His dealings with these men, Jesus pointed out yawning gulfs in their understanding of God's Word. But at bottom, the trouble here was their trouble all along. Self-reliance hid from them the salvation of God, and self-reliance hid from them the message of God. This was what Jesus meant when He gave thanks for the way in which what was obscure to them, 'the wise', was revealed to babes. The humble man, however unlearned, is not only potentially, but *already* a better student of God's Word than one who, though scholarly, is proud. Lesson One is therefore very plain. Every Christian has needed God's help to understand the message that has made him what he is; and he needs that help continually to understand the message which will make him grow in grace.

On the other hand, it is equally a fallacy to think that sincere prayer short-circuits the need for careful study. It is sometimes suggested that devotional reading of the Bible and academic study of the Bible are two separate, though both legitimate, activities. This is an error. Of course, it is true that there are passages which one knows well, and whose meaning is not in doubt, to which one may return for help and inspiration. Perhaps spadework on such passages has been done long since and we can reap successive harvests from them. But the spadework is essential. And those too lazy to do it stand to reap a thin harvest or a harvest of tares. A good sermon consists of both exposition and application. The fighting officer needs both to decode and to act upon the signal he receives. And in the same way the proper devotional use of the Bible should rest on an unashamedly *intellectual* grasp of its message. Any alternative position is selling out to sentimentality or even magic.

So much we must say about feeding upon the Word of God. But it is not enough to leave the matter there. The assimilation of Scripture is only the beginning of the fulfilment of God's purpose for it in the life of the believer.

The Bible falls into two parts: law and gospel. The distinction is reflected in the division between Old and New Testament. But there is a sense in which there is much gospel in the Old Testament and much law in the New. What I mean is that Scripture has a double thrust: an imperative thrust and an indicative thrust; what God tells us to do, and what God has done.

In so far as God's Word is law, it is, as Jesus Himself graphically explained, the folly of the man who builds his house on sand to take it in at the ear and not express it in the act. Bible study ought therefore to have a practical outcome, because if it is being done properly it can serve only to open our eyes to things that God is telling us to do.

But although we speak about law and gospel rather than gospel and law, when we look at the Bible as a whole, we find that while there is a sense in which what God has done is an answer to the problems entailed by what He has told us to do, it is also true that from the beginning obedience to the law was intended as the response to God's gracious activity. And from the Christian's point of view what God has done is good news. Yet as long ago as Elisha's day, the Bible spelt out the logical requirement of those who were in possession of good news. The lepers at the gate of the besieged city of Samaria who decided to chance their arm and surrender to the Syrians found their camp, when they reached it, empty of all but booty; they knew then that it was their duty to tell others, the king's household (2 Ki. 7:9). What then is expected of those who have discovered the unsearchable riches of Christ? Are not the tidings of the day too good for them to hold their peace? The message which burned in the bones of Jeremiah was a message of coming judgment. If he could not withstand the heat and pressure of that uncomfortable trust, but was compelled to declare it, should there not be a heat and pressure in the bones of those commissioned with the comfortable words of Christ's gospel?

No doubt it is true that, in large measure, the clearer our understanding of the Word of God, the greater our desire to transmit it to others. But equally certainly it would be unwise to rely on this fact. It is fitting that we should pray for opportunities to explain to people round us what we discover for ourselves, and for clarity in conveying it, so that the thrill that very often comes to one engaged in Bible study may register its impression on others.

Everything that God gives us is a trust: possessions, talents, wife, children—everything. But at the top of the list comes what God says to us. The point is often made in the New Testament that a preacher is a steward of the message given to him. It is not his to sell or to adulterate; he must neither add to it nor subtract from it. It is his only to pass on, to expound, as one might squeeze oil from nuts, or mint coins from gold. Conversely, just as it is clear to anyone called to preach where he must get his message from, so it is clear to anyone who gets a message from there, that he is called to preach it. For to whom did God ever speak in the whole course of the Bible without also wanting to speak through him?

The life and teaching of Christ is therefore a parable. He is

God's word to man. But in practice He had both to assimilate God's word in Scripture and to convey it to others. To study the Bible as a Christian is to walk in His steps. There is a taking in and a giving out. The one involves much self-imposed discipline, and the other may involve much suffering at the hands either of circumstances or of other people: Paul was both shipwrecked and stoned. But if both the study and the declaration are essential factors in the task of the Christian sower, and if the study involves effort as certainly as the declaration risks danger, the psalmist's promise sustains us:

> 'A man may go out weeping,
>   carrying his bag of seed;
> but he will come back with songs of joy,
>   carrying home his sheaves' (Ps. 126:6, NEB).